ALSO BY

MAGGIE LANE

Needlepoint by Design

MORE NEEDLEPOINT
BY DESIGN

MAGGIE LANE

MORE NEEDLEPOINT BY DESIGN

CHARLES SCRIBNER'S SONS / NEW YORK

To Myles

ACKNOWLEDGMENT

I wish to express my heartfelt thanks to two people for their invaluable help in the creation of this book: to Florence Gustafson who made available to me many volumes from her extensive library of Oriental art, and to Elinor Parker for editing my work.

Contents

(*v*)

COLOR PLATES   following pages 54, 134

Foreword

In the late fifties my wife and I were calling on a newly arrived addition to my staff in their charming home and were especially taken with the dining room chairs. The seats were needlepoint, each a different bouquet of flowers. The young officer told us with much pride that his talented wife had done them. On the way home I suggested to Dinny, my wife, that she start such a project so she purchased two canvases. Watching her I got the urge to try, and found it most relaxing as well as something to do while "watching" television.

Not wishing it known what I did in my spare time it was a well-kept secret until one of my Commanders surprised me one evening when he dropped by to deliver a dispatch. Instead of being amused he evinced great interest and inquired as to where he could buy the materials. About a month later we were invited to his home and he proudly displayed a picture in needlepoint of a China Clipper in full sail which he had designed and done himself. This was the first of many creations by this six foot four Navy Commander.

Over the years I have found needlework just what I needed to unwind from the pressures of my varied complex commands. During the 1961 Berlin Crisis my staff was ordered to the Eastern Atlantic with eight destroyers, a tanker, and an aircraft carrier. As there were no regularly planned operations requiring long hours of flying, as was usual, we had time to fill waiting for something to happen. Therefore many hobbies not usually seen on board surfaced and I was surprised to note the number of he-men doing handwork that we think only women do—needlework and rug-hooking especially.

While on duty in Washington several years ago a mutual friend sent me a copy of Maggie Lane's fascinating *Needlepoint by Design*. I had not done any research on this subject and was sorry to have missed so much. Being in the Navy I became interested to discover some of the beautiful needle-

work that sailors in the nineteenth century had done. With many leisure hours between those of great activity they spent many of these decorating their duffle bags with pictures of ships, nautical designs and scenes of ports they had visited. Excellent examples of this work are displayed in the Naval Museum, Washington, D.C., and the Smithsonian Institution. With this background of American naval artistry I am now proud to show off my needlepoint and highly recommend this handwork as a soothing hobby with the added pleasure and satisfaction of personal creativity.

My big regret is that I did not have Maggie Lane's excellent book sooner to inspire and guide me. However, she has my sincere appreciation for continuing her beautiful work and putting the results in a new book for all of us to enjoy and share.

GEORGE P. KOCH
Rear Admiral, U. S. Navy

MORE NEEDLEPOINT
BY DESIGN

1

EVEN though we call it needle*work*, needlepoint is fun. If it were not, it would never have achieved its present popularity. I am sure that no one who has opened this book, and has read this far, ever picks up his or her canvas with a sigh. This may be partly because needlepoint is almost like a living thing. From first stitch to last it grows, and therefore fascinates almost everyone who has chosen it as a pastime. It has been said that there are two kinds of needle-workers: the minority, those who will never finish their first canvases; and the rest of us who go on—canvas after canvas—finally to become addicts.

To some, needlepoint is a tranquilizer. To others it is a form of occupational therapy, an aid, perhaps, to keeping nervous hands from lighting up another cigarette. To me, however, it is a vital form of creation as well as recreation, and it is also a means of fulfilling my need to use my precious time productively. Hardly a day goes by that I do not spend three or four hours designing graphs or working with needle and canvas in hand. So that when night falls I can say I have not wasted the daylight hours; I have produced something tangible; and it is always my hope that I have added a bit of beauty to the world.

Perhaps my preoccupation with the productive use of time stems from the fact that my parents were missionaries. They served in China, where I was born and grew up.

Those years in the Orient were perilous times. Before I had reached my teens China was heading straight for a crisis. Since the early thirties, tensions of war had been steadily mounting, and at the end of that decade the American Consul in Peking began urging all United States citizens to return to America. By March of 1941, the spring before Pearl Harbor, the international situation had become so dangerous for Americans in China that

my parents decided to heed the Consul's pleas. In haste, then, they closed our mission house where they left most of our precious belongings, because they thought we would all be returning some day.

Once in this country, Mother therefore had to buy furniture. And among the many articles she bought was a dining table and a set of six chairs. None of us cared for the ugly matlassé that covered the slip seats, so Mother bought six needlepoint canvases. On each of these, professional drones had already worked the central wreath of flowers. Mother hoped that she, my sister and I, even though absolute novices, could learn how to do needlepoint, and work the backgrounds in a reasonable length of time. To this end she had also bought pounds of faded-navy tapestry wool.

Well, that was my introduction to needlepoint. My sister quickly learned the half-cross stitch, and taught it to Mother and me. We then began our separate canvases. I remember with chagrin the way my stitches sloped sometimes in one direction, sometimes in another. But I continued to work in a desultory fashion for a period of several months. At the end of that time I had finished less than a quarter of the seat cover. Suddenly the tedium of the work daunted me. I threw down the distasteful assignment and resolved firmly never to work another needlepoint stitch. My sister, too, had found working on her canvas less than fascinating. That left Mother alone to finish all six chair covers. (Which she did!)

As soon as I finished college I left home and journeyed to New York to become a working girl. Paying the rent took a good part of my salary. But I was happy and content until a strong nostalgia for things Chinese began to trouble me. Then, the idea of owning an oriental rug gradually grew to be an obsession. I began to wake up each morning wanting to see one by my sofa-bed the moment I opened my eyes. I wanted to put my bare feet on warm wool when I stepped out of bed. I wanted to enjoy the comfort of its presence and serene design as I moved around

(2)

my room. I shopped about but found even the smallest ones costly, much more than I could afford.

In my life I have so often found the "do-it-yourself" solution the only answer to many such situations. I realized that if ever I *were* to own a Chinese rug I would have to make it myself. Once I had accepted this fact, I knew I would have to break my vow about needlepoint, since its flat stitches were so eminently suitable for reproducing the smooth surfaces of worn antique carpets.

The New York Public Library was my first stop. There I found many volumes devoted to Chinese rugs, and pored over them avidly. At last, among all the many beautiful designs, I found a picture of a simple rug that I particularly liked, and which I could see would adapt itself well to needlepoint.

The library offers, among many services, this important one: they will photostat on request any page of any book—except pages in books too rare, too old, or too fragile. The library will even enlarge the stats. I asked for 8″ x 10″ prints. A few days later these arrived in the mail.

I then went out and bought two yards of gros-point canvas thirty-six inches in width, a roll of brown wrapping paper, a bottle of india ink, a pen, and a few water-color brushes. On the paper I roughed out the Ming Dynasty design. I drew it 30″ wide and 60″ long, a size tailored to fit the canvas while leaving a 3″ border on the sides, and 6″ at either end for blocking and hemming. When I had outlined and inked in the design on the paper, I laid my canvas over it and, reading through the scrim, tried to trace the pattern on the ecru threads. For me this was a blinding process. I have always enjoyed painting on smooth white oil-canvas, but I found that I detested painting on a brown sieve. Even so I went on until I observed that the swastika border was not working properly on the canvas—the drawing on paper had not been scaled for the number of canvas threads to the inch. I knew then that I had no choice but to draw, on the canvas, one correct swastika, then repeat it by count all the way around the

(3)

rug, swastika after swastika, turning the corners properly, and making the corrected border fit within the limits I had originally planned.

So I set to my task. I drew one swastika, then another, then another, on and on. Try it yourself some time. Those twisted creatures nearly drove me mad. But my desire for a finished rug kept me going. I remember my suspense as I came down the final stretch hours later, hoping against hope that the last lines would join the first without any visible jogs. Fortunately they did.

The Ming rug had a pair of intertwining dragons in its center. In the long field divided by this motif two symmetrical sprays of peony flowers and leaves faced each other, and a key fret filled each of the four corners. Having already set my course toward a counted design I decided that in my rug nothing less than absolute perfection would now do. I knew I was not going to achieve it by the tracing method. I also knew that any mistakes I made in drawing on the canvas would be impossible to erase. So I went out to buy several large sheets of fresh, clean graph paper on which an eraser could easily correct any of my miscalculations. I glued these sheets of paper together to make a large piece on which I charted the length and width of the rug as already counted on the canvas. Within this border I graphed each element of the design. And I have been graphing ever since.

2

During all the many years that I have since spent designing graphs for needlepoint, I have found myself guided by a fairly rigid set of rules. These might be termed my philosophy of needlepoint. With the idea that these precepts may be helpful to you I set them down here.

Before any designer begins to sketch a plan, whether it be for a complex skyscraper or a simple canvas for a pillow, a clear objective is essential. The artist must first decide whether he wishes to create something of classic beauty, something whimsical, something elegant, or something with what I like to call "hard chic." This decision shapes the course he will follow, and sets his first limitations.

Limitations are, in fact, what shape everything we make or do. To be specific, needlepoint has its limitations. It also has many assets. But I shall first list its qualities on the debit side, for only when we recognize these traits and accept them can we achieve freedom within the limits they set.

The act of stitching a piece of needlepoint is a time-consuming one. The end product, however, is insured of a long life. We know of works that have lasted for centuries. This limitation—of being time-consuming—should logically impose on us a desire to select only the best when we go out to buy a design on which we will spend our precious hours. So many pictures painted on needlepoint canvas are not worthy of the length of time required to work them in wool. We should pass them by and accept only designs of timeless beauty that will continue to please, year after year. It also follows automatically that harsh, blatant colors, those in fashion at the moment—those that will soon become dated—should also be put aside in favor of colors we can live with, but most particularly, *colors, themselves, that can live with each other!*

Another limitation is set for us by the nature of the canvas on which we work our stitches. The strict grid of horizontal and vertical threads does not give us the freedom given the men who work with mosaic tiles, each of which can be tailored to fit a space. But I like to think of needlepoint and mosaics as parallel crafts. And I would like to point out here that, even with their greater freedom, mosaic workers have traditionally created highly stylized designs suitable to the medium.

Worked on the canvas grid, all basket weave or continental

needlepoint stitches slant in the same direction. This could be considered a limitation. Let us say we wish to work stitches outlining a full circle. Half the outline will follow a smooth curve. The other half will give a slightly jagged, saw-toothed appearance because the stitches slant at right angles to the curve. So only an *illusion* of a curve can be achieved, and it is best appreciated when seen from a little distance.

However, the strict canvas grid offers an advantage as well as the limitation just described. Needlepoint is admirably suited to linear and geometric designs.

Needlepoint wools are available to us in a wide range of colors. Many of these are shaded rather smoothly from light to dark. Nevertheless, as a medium for creating illusions, woolen stitches are clumsy when compared with the facility of film in a camera or the subtleties paint and brush on oil-canvas can produce. Therefore needlepoint should be used neither for portraits nor for trompe l'oeil effects where the finest gradations of shading and line are required. We should never torture a medium by asking too much of it. Instead we should accept and work within the limits of whatever medium we select to serve us.

So much for limitations. Now for assets:

Needlepoint is a very sturdy medium. Usually worked in wool on cotton canvas—two fibers of admitted strength—it will undoubtedly outlast its maker and continue to survive wear for a long time. For this reason I believe that needlepoint should always be designed to serve a functional as well as a decorative purpose. Another reason I adhere to this rule follows: it has been said that the difference between the fine arts and the minor arts lies in the fact that fine art serves no purpose except that of being decorative. Needlepoint is only a minor art. Therefore it should never aspire to being purely decorative. Its primary purpose should be functional.

When selecting a medium for design the artist does well to bear in mind the use to which the final product will be put. It would be ridiculous, for example, for anyone to tie up a gift

package with something having the tensile strength of a steel band. Obviously a softer, more supple ribbon would serve the purpose better.

People often suggest to me that I design needlepoint for items they think I have never before considered. These usually run to hat bands, ties, or vests. I am always grateful for any help I may be given. But people don't seem to realize that narrow bands offer little room for designing, and darts in bulky needlepoint do not enhance it, nor the vest of which it is made. But these are not the reasons why I have never designed any of the above listed things. I have designed luggage straps, suspenders, belts, even shoes. Each of these items offers little room for pattern, but each *does* serve a functional purpose even before it serves a decorative one. It holds something up, or in, or protects it from hurt, and therefore must be made of sturdy stuff. But hat bands, ties and vests perform no such services. They merely decorate the wearer at the same time they are scratching him and surely making him uncomfortable. A softer fabric would seem so much more suitable for such things. And framed needlepoint pictures, behind glass, hanging on the wall!!! This *is* a misuse of the medium. Here I repeat: NEEDLEPOINT IS STURDY and should be used only where strong materials are needed. If you want a picture for your wall, paint one!

This rule—that needlepoint must serve a functional purpose—sounds rigid. It is. One exception to it, however, must be allowed. Tapestries were first made centuries ago to serve two purposes: one, admittedly purely decorative; the other, the more practical one of insulating cold, clammy walls, and slightly warming the air in frigid halls of old stone castles.

The design on the cover of my first book, *Needlepoint by Design,* was conceived originally as a rug for the front hall of our New York apartment. I intended the dragon to guard the entrance door. The rug was stitched on gros-point canvas with heavy, durable wool. But when I had finished it, my husband would allow no one to set foot on it. I must admit I was flattered,

but at the same time I was dismayed because of the firm stand I have always taken against strictly decorative needlepoint. However, rather than roll up my rug and put it away where it could serve no purpose whatsoever—not even a decorative one—I had no choice but to make an exception to my rule. So now the rug, as a purely decorative and needlessly sturdy tapestry, hangs on our living-room wall—which I hasten to point out is neither cold, clammy, nor made of stone.

3

NEEDLEPOINT should never look like something it is not. It should not look like a piece of fabric cut from a bolt. It should be unique. Why else go to all the trouble of making it? Why not instead just cut off a length of material? I know you are familiar with the kind of needlework where masses of flowers crawl right up to the edges of the piece and would go beyond except that their petals and leaves have been cruelly lopped off and mutilated. This variety of design—and all-over patterns with no borders—might as well have been woven by a machine. With all the freedom of choice open to us when we begin a piece of needlework, why should we not select a design, or better yet, create one of our own with a specific purpose, shape and use in mind?

Although needlepoint is usually thought of as two dimensional, it can also be used to cover solid objects. This, of course, requires a different approach to design, and is automatically more complex, since the area to be worked includes four sides as well as the focal one: the front, or the top. But flat or cubed, the limitations of the area to be worked present us with definite outlines: a circle, a square, a rectangle or octagon, to name a few flat shapes, and a cube, a cylinder or a table with four legs, to

name a few solid ones. Each gives us its own geographical limits which become our outlines. We must work within these frameworks.

Let us first consider the flat surface with its single outline. To me this becomes the outer edge of a frame. Since I am a painter I design borders around all my flat needlepoint surfaces because I like to see pictures in frames. Even while at work on a painting I will often slip it into a handy frame just to see how it will ultimately look. The painting will suddenly take on a finished appearance because the frame surrounds it. The right line in the styling of a woman's hair will work the same magic for her face. Of course, the wrong frame can ruin a picture just as the wrong coiffure can destroy the illusion of beauty.

When I design the more complex needlepoint canvases intended to cover solid objects, I usually think of the top—or front—surface as the picture and the four visible sides as the frame. I therefore consider it unnecessary to put anything but a simple, ribbon-like band around the edge of the picture, because the intricate kind of pattern I generally use in my borders will always be visible around the picture except when it is viewed head-on.

Any good design must work well within the two limits that I have already mentioned: it uses its medium properly, and also uses to good advantage its physical, or geographical, boundaries.

Good design also has another quality: *it is essentially simple*. Those who paint designs on needlepoint canvas should never forget this fact. A good design should carry its message quickly and directly across a reasonable distance, just as a poster does. If it accomplishes this purpose and clearly says "flower" or "bird" or whatever, the viewer, being intrigued, may draw nearer, even to where he can make a minute inspection. At this point a good design will reward him with subtleties not discernable at a distance—the delicious and delightful business of pertinent detail.

Needlepoint is therefore most successful when flat areas of color are used, and where subtle lines within these areas tell

(9)

the story of drapery folds or of contour. A multitude of stitches are also available to us for use within these areas when we want to indicate changes of texture. Shading, if used at all, should be simple and direct, and in close tones. For this in itself makes for subtlety, but a subtlety suitable to the medium.

4

In my first book I made available to you, in graph form, a group of related designs. For a central motif most of them had an aquatic creature or an insect of some sort, and a different border surrounded almost every graph. Once the book went to the publishers I felt that I must go on to designing another kind of needlework.

During the summer of 1970 I met Mrs. Robert Lantz. She is an artist in needlework, and in the course of time I saw some of her work. She has created the most beautiful needlepoint samplers I have ever seen. After seeing these squares I inevitably decided that *I* must learn to do all the stitches diagrammed in all the needlework books I could find. I also decided to work them up as a sampler. But I decided it must be one that would be useful as well as decorative. A chessboard was my solution. Mrs. Lantz told me what kind of canvas and materials she had used in her exquisite works. She told me that #14 canvas was best for embroidery stitches and that she had used silk for her samplers. Her reason: the architecture of each stitch is more readily visible when the thread used is smooth rather than fuzzy. She told me that for most stitches she had used only five of the seven threads that cling together in a strand.

Armed with this invaluable information I bought a piece of #14 canvas and several skeins of silk, three of beige and three

of white, because I knew from experience that all intricate stitches show up better in pale tones than in dark ones.

I marked off my canvas into squares, sixty-four of them, each measuring 24 threads by 24 threads. I chose this thread count because it is divisible by 2, 3, 4 and 6, the numbers of threads crossed in most of the embroidery stitches. Then I began to work.

My plan was to place next to each other boxes of stitches that would contrast with, and therefore enhance, each other.

In making this sampler, along with the fun of learning a new vocabulary of stitches, I was also preparing for myself a chart of finished squares that would help me in choosing for a design one stitch or another whose texture most closely resembled the texture I wished to simulate: tree bark, or fish scales, for example. In none of the books to which I had referred had I found clear photographs of the various stitches. I had found only diagrams. So I had no idea what each stitch would look like until I had actually worked it up.

Not all classic needlework stitches can be worked on mono canvas. One must use Penelope canvas in order to be able to make some of them. So, filling 64 squares of mono canvas without repeating a single texture became a challenge. By the time I approached the last row I had run out of stitches suitable for work on mono canvas. So I resorted to combining stitches already used. In doing so I was able to make different surface patterns. I think I may even have invented a texture or two.

If you turn to pages 14 and 15, you will see the results of my research—and the diagrams for the stitches used in the sampler.

The rows of boxes have been numbered and lettered and the name of each stitch therefore appears with a number and a letter beside it. A bibliography of reference books is attached.

In working decorative stitches I have found that all stitches crossing the canvas at a 45° angle require thinner thread than those stitches crossing the canvas horizontally and vertically. I also found that a "sampler" canvas was handy. I tried out each

new stitch on it. In this way I could determine how thick the yarn or thread should be for adequate coverage. And sometimes I found that I needed a "filler" stitch between the ornamental stitches to enhance the appearance of the work. (In this regard of course you must be the judge.) Only after these experiments and decisions had been made would I work the stitch on my chessboard canvas. AT ALL TIMES I TRIED TO KEEP MY THREAD FROM TWISTING.

I really do not know why I waited so long to try out the decorative stitches. The only answer that seems at all probable to me is that I was intimidated by their appearance of complexity. When I actually got down to brass tacks I found that the different stitches are simply various ways of covering the canvas. By that I mean that the basket weave covers the canvas with a short stitch slanting from lower left to upper right. It is one of the most time-consuming of all the stitches because one must make a stitch for every intersection of canvas threads. The decorative stitches, however, show longer stretches of thread, some sets of which make fans, some make crosses, some simply lie next to each other producing a satiny finish. But almost all of them work up faster than the basket weave!

On the following pages you will find the diagrams I have prepared. I have made all of them on uniform canvas so that the size of each stitch is readily apparent. I have worked in white on black because I believe this to be the most dramatic way of showing a pattern.

THE STITCHES

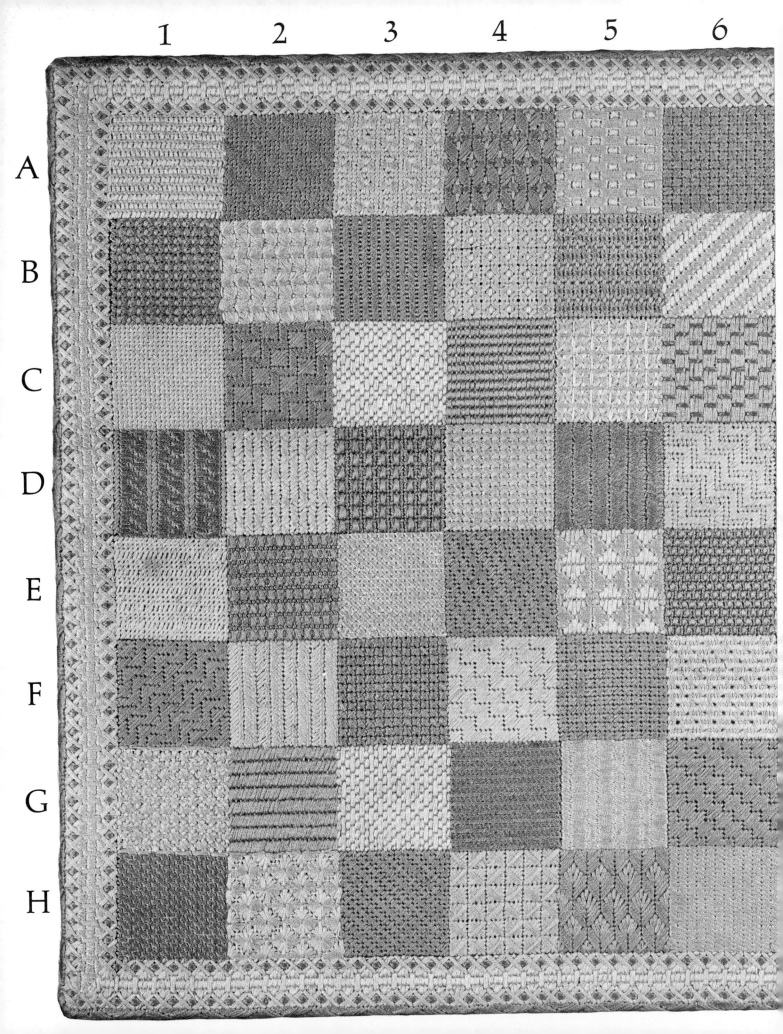

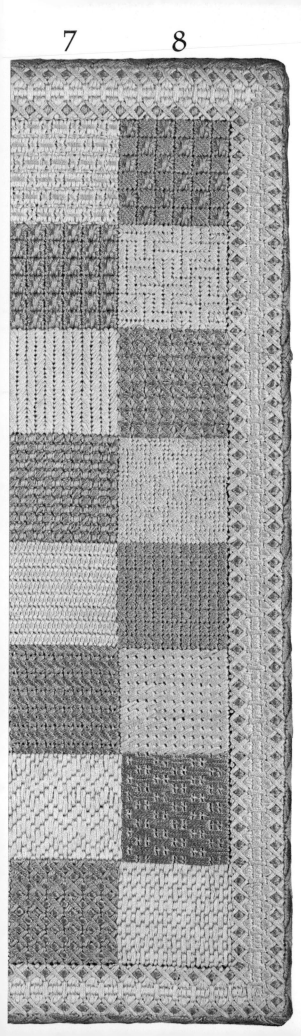

Key to Stitches on Chessboard

Those with * are my own.

A 1   The simple buttonhole, or blanket, stitch.

A 2   The checker stitch.

A 3   The small eyelet combined with continental stitch.

A 4   The satin stitch combined with double straight cross stitch.*

A 5   The old Florentine stitch with a cross stitch over the short threads.*

A 6   The Mosaic stitch turned around back and forth, alternately.*

A 7   The oblong cross stitch with back stitch alternating with five upright satin stitches tied down with one back stitch.*

A 8   The double Leviathan stitch and Scotch stitch alternating.

B 1   The Montenegrin cross stitch.

B 2   The ray stitch.

B 3   The stem stitch.

B 4   The mosaic stitch, halved and turned, combined with the upright cross stitch.*

B 5   The oblong cross stitch with back stitch and filler.

B 6   The damask darning stitch.

B 7   The double Leviathan stitch.

B 8   The grounding of satin stitch in form of a cross.

C 1   The basket weave stitch.

C 2   The Byzantine stitch with Scotch stitch.

C 3   Hungarian ground or Point d'Hongrie stitch.

C 4   The straight Gobelin with long padding stitch underneath.

(15)

C 5　The square eyelet stitch with horizontal and vertical filler.

C 6　Algerian filling with horizontal filler stitch.

C 7　The satin stitch.

C 8　The two-sided Italian or arrow head cross stitch.

D 1　The satin stitch with continental stitch reversed.

D 2　The perspective stitch.

D 3　The triple cross stitch.*

D 4　The Greek stitch worked in one direction only.

D 5　The fern stitch.

D 6　The Jacquard stitch.

D 7　Two cross stitches with filler stitch between.

D 8　A variation of the Moorish stitch.

E 1　The interlocking Gobelin, long and short, 2-2-3; 2-2-3.

E 2　The double stitch.

E 3　The upright cross stitch.

E 4　The cashmere stitch done diagonally.

E 5　The triangle stitch.

E 6　The Smyrna cross stitch.

E 7　The knotted stitch.

E 8　The cashmere stitch.

F 1　The Milanese stitch.

F 2　The fishbone stitch.

F 3　The cross stitch tramé.

F 4　The Byzantine stitch.

F 5　The Mosaic stitch.

F 6　The rococo stitch.

F 7　The Greek stitch worked back and forth. See D 4.

F 8　The oblique Slav stitch.

G 1　The double straight cross stitch.

G 2　The slanting Gobelin stitch.

G 3　The Hungarian embroidery stitch.

G 4　The knitting stitch.

G 5　The darning stitch.

G 6　The Scotch stitch done diagonally.

G 7　The bargello, or flame, stitch.

G 8　The old Florentine stitch on its side.

H 1　The brick stitch.

H 2　The diamond eyelet stitch.

H 3　The Florentine mosaic stitch.

H 4　The Scotch stitch.

H 5　The leaf stitch.

H 6　The encroaching oblique stitch.

H 7　The double cross stitch.

H 8　The Parisian embroidery stitch.

To Make the Chessboard

Bind off a piece of #14 canvas, measuring 22″ x 22″. (If you wish to do only the 64 squares, count off 192 threads by 192 threads. Box them into squares of 24 threads by 24 threads.) The boxing band measures 12 threads in depth. The face of the chessboard measures 216 threads by 216 threads, including the border.

A 1

The simple button hole, or blanket, stitch is worked from left to right. Begin at the bottom left hand corner of the square.

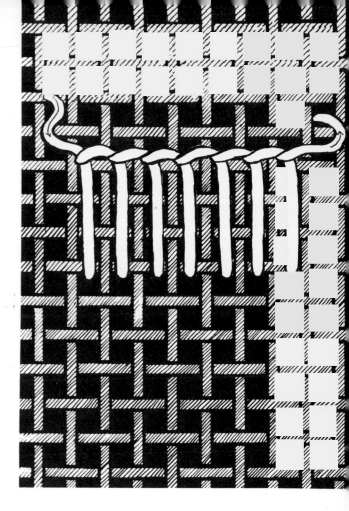

A 2

The checker stitch is a combination of the satin stitch and the basket weave in alternating squares covering three vertical and three horizontal canvas threads.

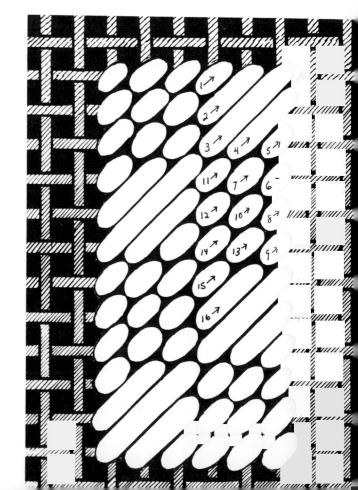

A 3

The small eyelet combines with a filler of continental stitches to make a charming pattern.

A 4

The satin stitch combines with the double straight cross stitch to make a handsome texture. Work vertical rows of satin stitch in groups of three, alternating the slant from group to group. Fill in blank spaces with the double straight cross stitch.

Dear Karen,

Here's that canvas for the top of the quilt. Cut it about 3 inches on the unfinished end of the quilt and then fold it over to the right side and topstitch around the scalloped edge. You can find a quilt maker to do it for me by putting in the yellow pages to see if one can find me a quilt one — that nice girl can that she did it — what she found around it. I was a member of a wonderful Christian person. I saw the top of a red sheet to make a protector for my flannel quilts. Hope you like the quilt. My top is late letter. Much love,
Grandma.

A 5

The old Florentine stitch with a cross stitch over the short threads produces a textured surface. Work a row of the old Florentine stitch first, then cover the short stitches with an oblique cross stitch and a vertical stitch. Work the second row in the same way. (See **G 8** for the old Florentine stitch.)

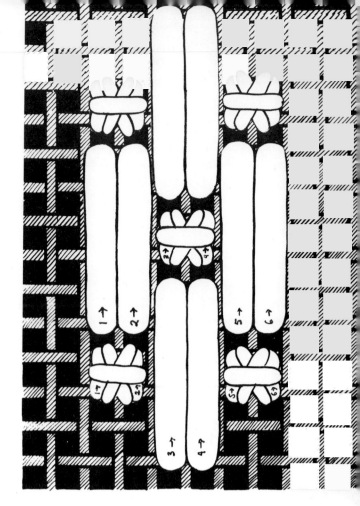

A 6

A variation of the mosaic stitch in which the three part stitch is slanted first one way, then the other. Begin at the top and work down. Work second row from bottom to top.

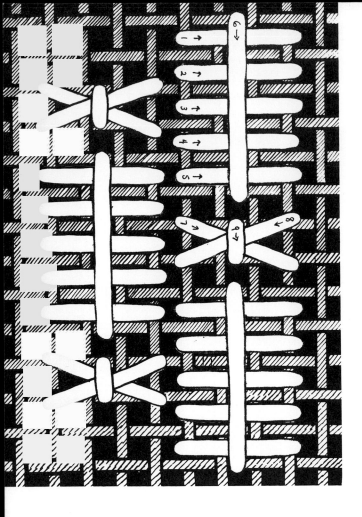

A 7

The oblong cross stitch (see **B 5**) with back stitch, alternating with five upright satin stitches tied down with one back stitch. Work from left to right in rows.

A 8

The double Leviathan stitch alternating with the large Scotch stitch makes a handsome checkerboard. Each stitch covers four horizontal and four vertical canvas threads.

DIAGRAM 1 shows the construction of one double Leviathan stitch. Make a large X stitch, then an oblique X over one arm of step one, then over the other arm of step one. Finally make an upright cross stitch over the whole preceding six strands. IF YOU END THE STITCH WITH A VERTICAL THREAD, AS SHOWN, END ALL SUCCEEDING STITCHES WITH A VERTICAL THREAD. IF YOU END THE STITCH WITH A HORIZONTAL THREAD, END ALL SUCCEEDING STITCHES WITH A HORIZONTAL THREAD.

A 8

DIAGRAM 2 shows a small section of the pattern produced by the combination of the Scotch stitch and the double Leviathan stitch.

B 1

The Montenegrin cross stitch works from left to right. The first arm of the first step of the stitch goes up over four canvas threads and to the right over eight canvas threads. The diagram gives directions for stitching each thread, and numbers the sequence you should follow.

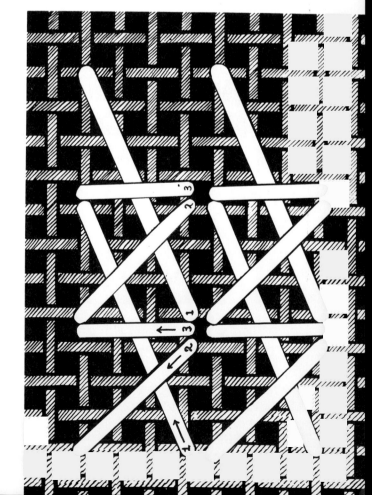

B 2

The ray stitch is worked most easily from right to left, as shown in the diagram. Turn the book and the canvas for the next row.

B 3

The stem stitch is worked in vertical rows of short oblique satin stitches slanting from upper right to lower left for one row, then from lower left to upper right for the next row. Vertical rows of back stitching cover the canvas threads between the rows of satin stitch.

B 4

The mosaic stitch, halved and turned, and combined with the upright cross stitch is worked in up and down rows. Work the rows of halved mosaic stitch first, then fill in the empty spaces with the upright cross stitch.

B 5

The oblong cross stitch with back stitch and filler is worked in horizontal rows. Work from left to right when working the oblong cross stitch, and from right to left when working the filler stitch.

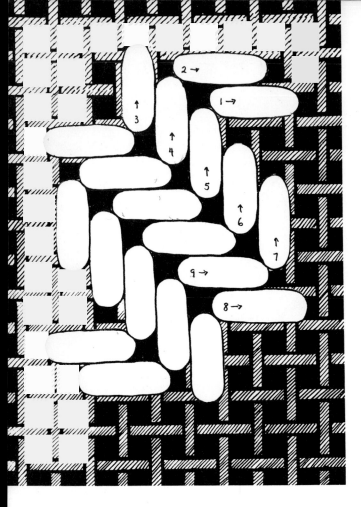

B 6

The damask darning stitch. This stitch requires a thick thread and is worked in diagonal rows of upright satin stitches.

B 7

The double Leviathan stitch: see diagram **A 8**.

B 8   (see below)

Background filler, worked in satin stitch.

C 1

The basket weave or the tent stitch, showing the right and the wrong way to work if you want to work with the weave of the canvas. The upper diagram shows the right way; the lower shows the wrong way: against the weave.

C 2

The Byzantine stitch with the Scotch stitch. The fragment shows only construction. Refer to the picture of the chess board to see the pattern that results.

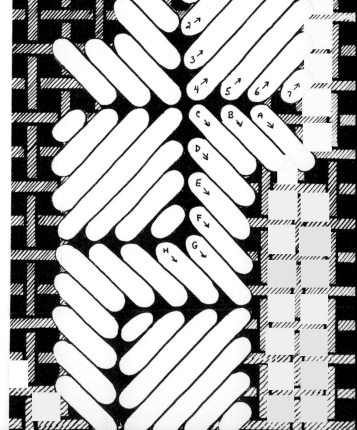

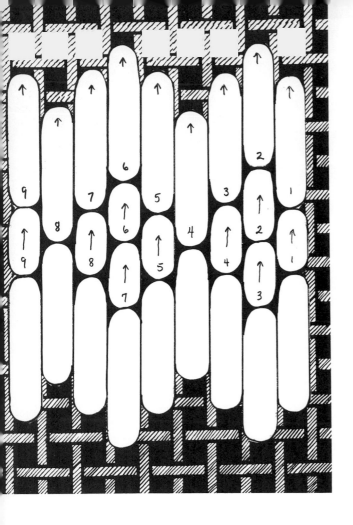

C 3

The Hungarian ground or Point D'Hongrie. Work the long stitches from right to left. Work the row of short stitches from right to left. Then work the second, row of long stitches, un-numbered in the chart. The long stitches cover four canvas threads, the short stitches cover two canvas threads. (If you always work the short stitches from bottom to top and work the upper of the two center short stitches first you can come back from left to right on the row of short stitches.)

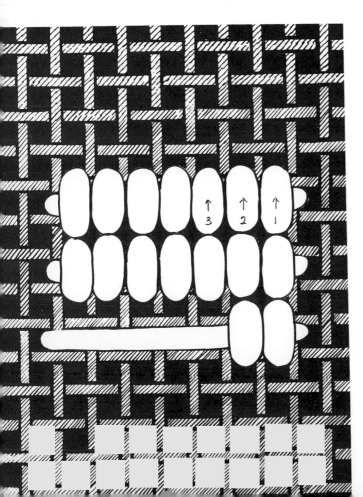

C 4

The straight Gobelin stitch over a long tramé stitch: work the long horizontal padding stitch to fill the space between every other horizontal canvas thread. Then work a row of short upright stitches to cover the tramé stitch and the two canvas threads between which the tramé stitch lies.

C 5

The square eyelet stitch with horizontal and vertical filler stitches. Work all the eyelet stitches as shown in the diagram. Then work the rows of vertical filler stitches, then the rows of horizontal filler stitches.

C 6

The Algerian filling with horizontal filler stitch is made up of vertical satin stitches in blocks of threes. These step up and down as shown. Each stitch covers three horizontal canvas threads. The horizontal filler stitches cover four vertical canvas threads.

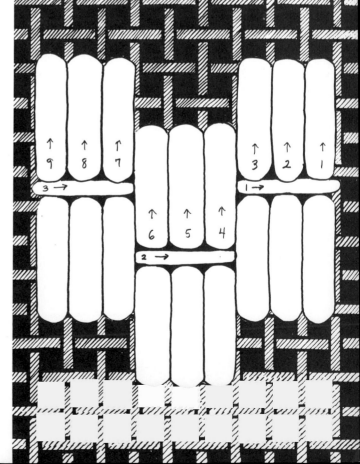

C 7

The satin stitch is made up of vertical rows of slanted stitches that go up over three canvas threads and either to the left or the right over two canvas threads. Work the stitch up and down, as shown on the diagram.

C 8

The two sided Italian, or arrowhead, cross stitch can be worked two ways. You can work steps one, two and three on each stitch, beginning at the left side of your canvas, and then work step four, the cross in the stitch, working from the right side of the canvas back to the left. Or you can finish each stitch as shown in the diagram, always working from left to right.

D 1

Horizontal satin stitch with continental stitch reversed. This works up into broad ribbon-like strips, eight vertical canvas threads wide.

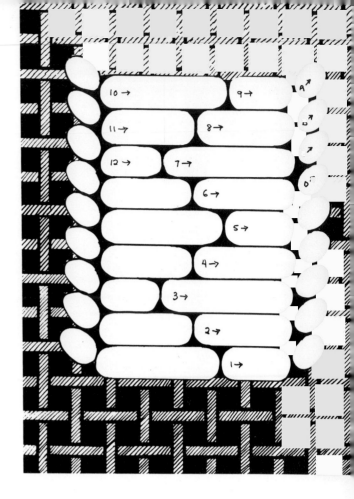

D 2

The perspective stitch works up best when started in the lower right hand corner. Work a vertical row of six satin stitches slanting up to the right, as shown on the diagram and numbered 1 to 6. Work the next row of six satin stitches parallel to the first row but slanting down to the right. Continue this horizontal band of vertical rows until you reach the left side of the canvas. Begin the next horizontal band made up of groups of vertical stitches, marked A to F on the diagram. Work them, then work G to L, and so on. Work across to the left side of the canvas. Then work the numbered row and the lettered row alternately.

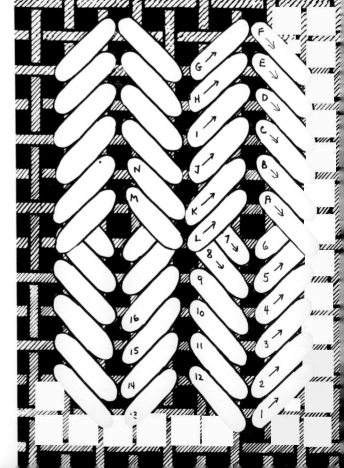

D 3

The triple cross stitch. The diagram shows the step by step construction of the stitch. End all stitches with the final stitch as shown on the diagram, step 6.

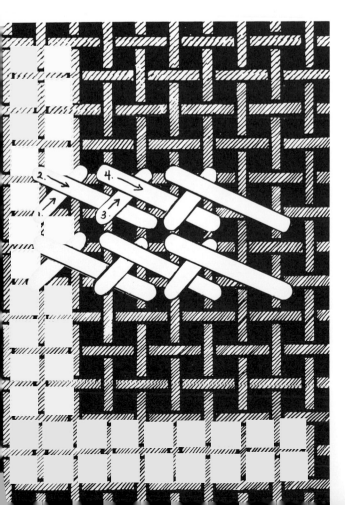

D 4

The Greek stitch. This is a long-armed cross stitch and can be worked two ways: from left to right only, or back and forth. In this case, work it from left to right only. When you get to **F 7** you will work it back and forth and produce a different looking texture.

D 5

The fern stitch. Work from top to bottom only. Fill in the space at the top of each row with a small back stitch.

D 6

The Jacquard stitch. This works up into a handsome diagonal zig-zag. It pulls the canvas out of shape somewhat so try not to pull your thread hard when you work this stitch.

D 7

Two cross stitches with filler stitch between. Work the upright and the cross stitch alternately, then fill in the horizontal, then the vertical, filler stitches.

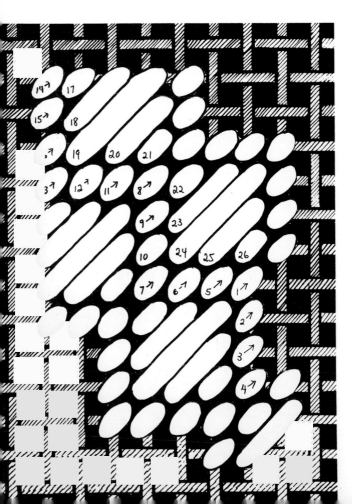

D 8

A variation of the Moorish stitch.

E 1

The interlocking Gobelin, long and short. Start at the lower right hand corner of the square. Make the first stitch up over three canvas threads and over one to the right. The next two stitches are up over only two canvas threads but still over one to the right. Continue this pattern of stitching until you reach the top of the square. Work the second vertical row immediately to the left of the first row, following the pattern already set.

E 2

The double stitch. This stitch alternates long and short cross stitches. Finish all stitches with the top stitch slanting in the same direction.

E 3

The upright cross stitch. This works up easily when you start in the lower right hand corner and work up diagonally toward the upper left hand corner. Work down as shown on the diagram, then work up again. Continue in this way until square has been filled.

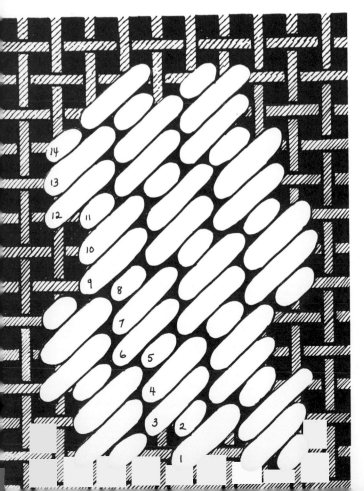

E 4

The cashmere stitch done diagonally. Work from lower right to upper left, then from upper left to lower right.

E 5

The triangle stitch. Work the long satin stitches to make the large square. Use thread thick enough to cover. Fill in the corners with little cross stitches worked in thinner thread.

E 6

The Smyrna cross stitch. The diagram shows the four steps in making the stitch; the two threads in the first, the x-shaped cross, and the two threads in the second, the +-shaped cross.

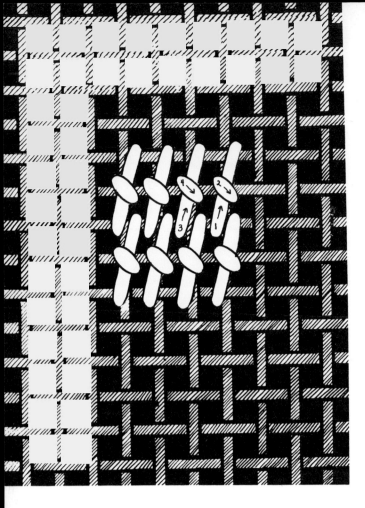

E 7

The knotted stitch. Work this stitch from the right to the left only.

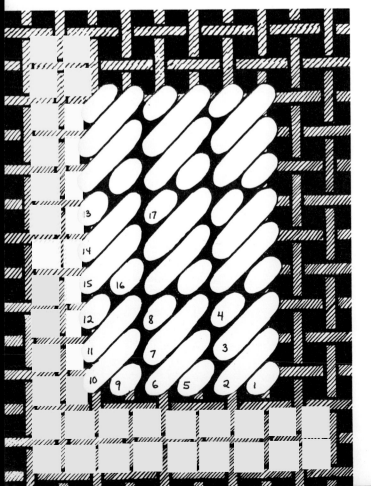

E 8

The cashmere stitch. Work this stitch in horizontal rows, back and forth as indicated in the diagram.

F 1

The Milanese stitch. Work this stitch from upper left to lower right to lower left and back up again as shown on the diagram. For a picture of the pattern it makes refer to the chess board.

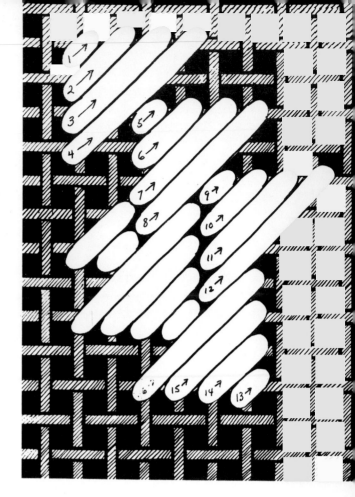

F 2

The fishbone stitch. Work this stitch in vertical rows, tying down each long diagonal stitch as you go along. You can work up one row, then down the next.

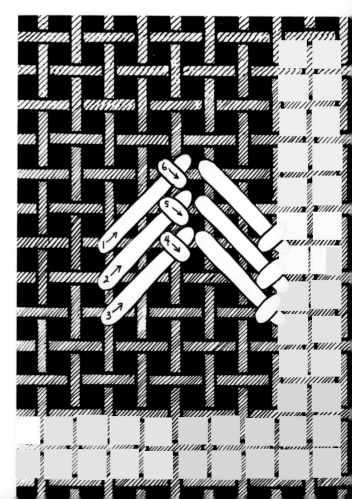

F 3

The cross stitch tramé. Work long padding stitches between every two sets of horizontal canvas threads. Work cross stitches over these long threads, making the first arm of the cross in one trip from right to left across the canvas. Make the second arm of the stitch in the second trip back from left to right.

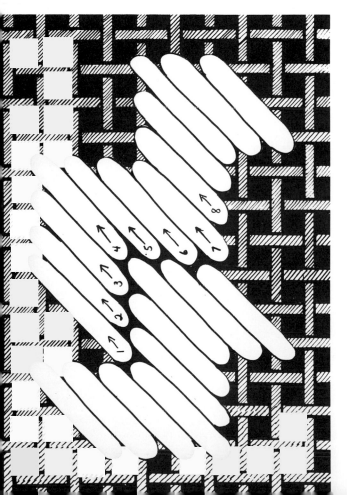

F 4

The Byzantine stitch. This stitch is worked in a zig-zag step from upper right to lower left, then back up again, the steps fitting into each other.

F 5

The mosaic stitch. This stitch is worked in vertical rows from top to bottom, or in horizontal rows from right to left.

F 6

The rococo stitch. This stitch looks complicated but is quite simple. I have numbered only the tie-down stitches, but their direction is most important. Pull them when you work, because part of the charm of the stitch is the holes that appear at top and bottom and at either side of each stitch. Work the stitches in diagonal rows.

THE STITCH REQUIRES A THINNER THREAD THAN MOST STITCHES.

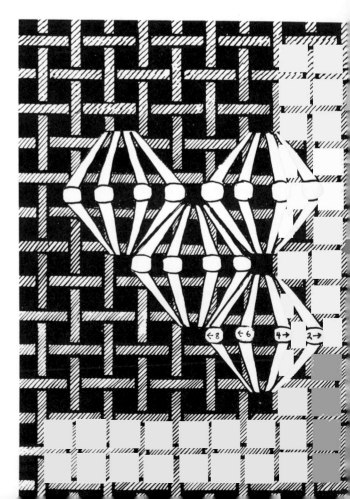

F 7

The Greek stitch—back and forth.

F 8

The oblique Slav stitch. This stitch works up best when done from left to right only. A half stitch, or filler should be put in at the ends of each row.

G 1

The double straight cross stitch. Make sure that all final threads cross the stitches in the same direction.

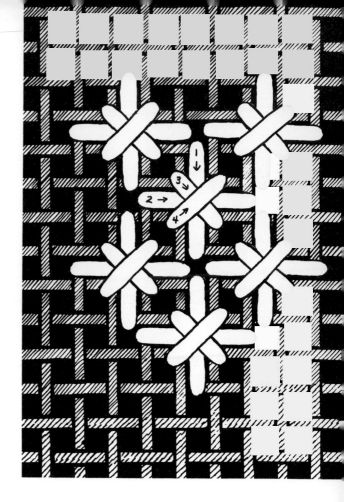

G 2

The slanting Gobelin stitch. This stitch works up to look like a rep fabric. Use heavy thread.

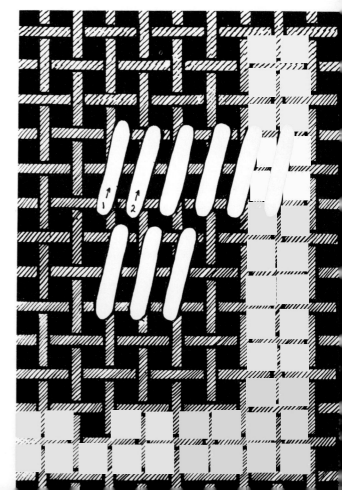

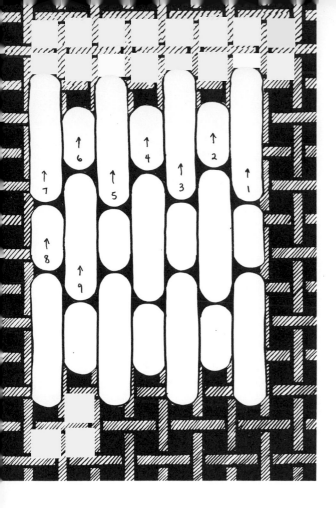

G 3

The Hungarian embroidery stitch. Work this stitch in horizontal rows from side to side. Use heavy thread.

G 4

The knitting stitch. Work from left to right only. Turn canvas and book for the second row. Fill end spaces with a half stitch.

G 5

The darning stitch. The stitch goes over two, under four, over two and under four canvas threads. Turn the canvas and, in the same holes, it goes over four, under two, over four and under two canvas threads. Repeat these two trips again in the same holes so that you have worked yarn twice in both the long and the short stretches. Repeat this pattern for each row. Each row fits between two horizontal canvas threads.

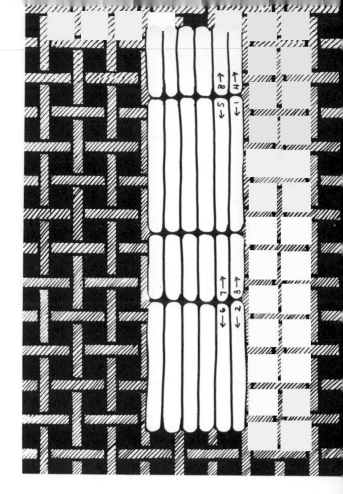

G 6

The Scotch stitch done diagonally. The diagram shows the construction of one row. For the pattern the stitch makes, refer to the chess board.

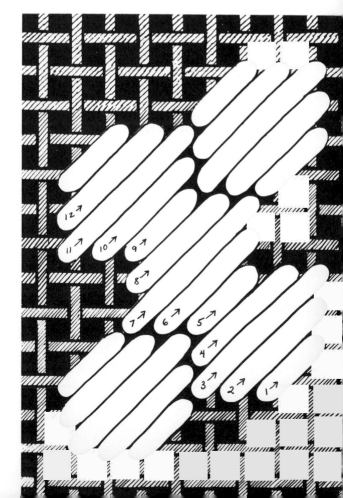

(43)

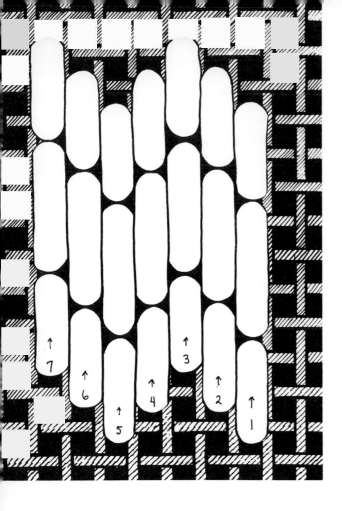

G 7

The bargello stitch. Work the horizontal rows of stitches, long for one row, short for the next, but both following an up and down movement as shown in the diagram.

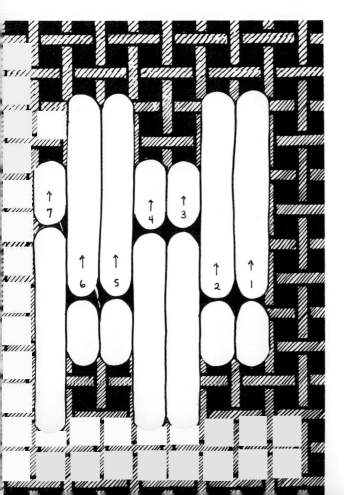

G 8

The old Florentine stitch. Work two long stitches over 6 canvas threads, then two short stitches over 2 canvas threads. Repeat all the way across the square. Return, fitting the second row to the first, as shown.

H 1

The brick stitch. This stitch needs fat thread. Work it up and down to produce a texture that looks like laid bricks. The first row is numbered. The second row is lettered. The back of the stitch looks like a basket-weave.

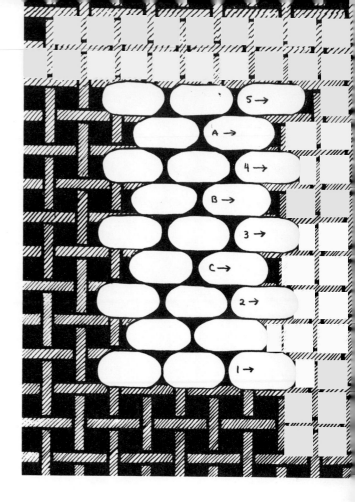

H 2

The diamond eyelet stitch. The only important thing to note here is the directional change that occurs at stitch nine. I suggest this change only for expediency's sake.

H 3

The Florentine mosaic stitch. Work this stitch in diagonal rows, up and down.

H 4

The Scotch stitch, a variation. Here the Scotch stitch is turned back and forth, and a tie-down is added, crossing at right angles to the direction of the threads in each Scotch stitch.

H 5

The leaf stitch. Each thread goes up over four canvas threads. The first three go to the right over three canvas threads. Stitch four goes to the right over two canvas threads, stitch five to the right over one canvas thread, and stitch six straight up, but *always up* over four canvas threads. Note the change in direction of stitch at seven. This is done only for expediency's sake. To begin a third leaf, start the first thread where number nine thread comes up, and where C thread goes down.

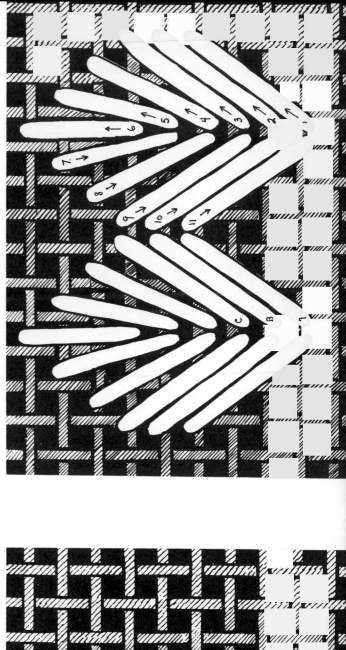

H 6

The encroaching oblique stitch. Work from left to right. Start work at the lower left hand corner of the canvas. Work the second row above the first, the third above the second, and so on.

H 7

The double cross stitch. Work the first arms of the big cross stitches all the way across the square. Then put in the second arms of the stitches on the return trip. Then fill in the empty places with the upright cross stitch.

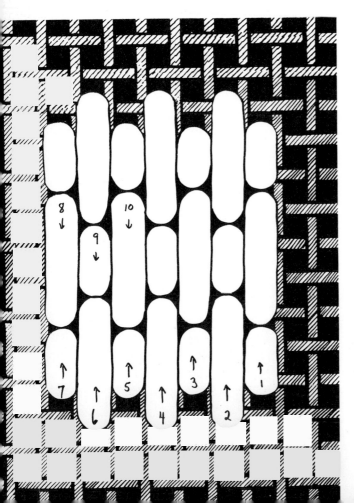

H 8

The Parisian embroidery stitch. Work this stitch in horizontal rows of long and short upright stitches.

This is the border for a corner of the chessboard.

5

Now let us get back to design, and to its actual bones.

Design is created by means of contrasting light and dark lines, areas or masses. A good design can be created without a single change in the color used, but never without changes in tonal value. A single color kind of design is called monochromatic. "Mono" means single, and "chroma" means color. But in monochromatic designs more than one tone of the single color *must* be used, since only contrast between light and dark results in pattern. A black and white photograph is a monochromatic design. Sculpture is also a form of monochromatic design. It is carved out of a material which is essentially of the same color throughout. But light, when falling on carved forms, rounds out convex masses, then turns to shadow when it loses itself in deep hollows. So it creates those changes in tonal value so necessary to design.

When I made my first pillow for a New York antique shop, the owner asked me to make it in black and white, using no color. Not realizing that he wanted me to use black and white alone without even a single in-between tone of gray, I made this first pillow, a stag beetle, in five almost monochromatic tones: tête de nègre, dark gray, taupe, light gray and ivory. The dealer liked it, but asked me to work thereafter in white and black only. This was a challenge, for he had, in his request, set for me the strictest limitations I could imagine unless it had been a request for a completely white or totally black piece of needlework where only changes in texture or stitches could create the pattern or design. I felt that he had in a sense asked me for a needlepoint sonnet or fugue. It was in response to his rigid limitations that I worked out several small-scale repeat patterns that I could use in black on white or vice-versa, whenever I wanted a medium gray tone. I also learned then how variety in the widths of adjoining border bands can enhance a design. And it was also at this time that I

worked out the two-tone zigzag border. In the first pillow I had given myself the luxury of five tones in the design and had worked them in the border in zigzag stripes shading from dark to light. But with only black and white to use I was momentarily stumped until I realized that I could create a kind of shading from dark to light by alternating wide and narrow bands at the same time as I alternated the black and white: first a black band three rows wide, next a single row of white, then a black band two rows wide, followed by a single row of white, a single black row, a single white row, then ever widening bands of white with single rows of black between.

In composing most of my designs I use three definite areas or concepts: the central motif, the surrounding field, and the border. For the first, the central motif, I prefer to work with objects that have interesting shapes. The crab, the lobster, and the frog all have very exciting contours when viewed from the top, as I chose to do them in my first book. I think of them as "espaliered" creatures. I designed them in this almost naive way because when seen from above, their outlines, each so characteristic of its owner, can be most easily identified. The creatures then immediately become universally recognized symbols. The butterfly, on the other hand, although clearly recognized by its outline when seen from almost any angle, has a less interesting "espaliered" shape. Therefore we must rely on interest within this basic outline—the contour of its wings. Nature has here given us plenty of help, offering to us a myriad different kinds of dotted, striped, and brilliantly colored patterns from which to choose. Even so I sometimes add further interest to my moths and butterflies by lengthening and coiling their antennae: for every designer *does*, after all, have artistic license.

I have one small but very important point I would like to make here in connection with artistic license: Each of us is partial to one or another style of painting or design. I myself love many kinds of art, but always find myself influenced by the Chinese when I design my needlepoint canvases. People often suggest to me that I should look elsewhere for my inspiration, lest I become

boring in my fidelity to the Orient. I tell them that what they ask is impossible. They might as well ask a leopard to cast off his spots in favor of stripes. However, the point I wish to make is that design is as old as the world, and there is nothing new in it, nothing that has not been tried before. A precious heritage from the past, art from the world over surrounds and influences every one of us. We owe it, and future generations, an obligation to be selective when we put our hands to making something that will outlast us by many years. That is why I suggest that when, for use in a design, you borrow an idea from the past, be sure you borrow only from the best.

In all fairness I feel that, since you have stayed with me this long, I should honor you with a confession: I have just recently made a second exception to the rigid set of rules listed earlier. Although I have been taking a stern and moral stand when preaching my philosophy of needlepoint, I now must admit that circumstances have at last forced me into making a purely decorative piece of needlework! More than that, I am now revelling in the forbidden sin of embroidering not just one but *two* panels intended for decoration and decoration alone!

When I realized it was the *only* answer to a very special need, the idea of "painting" with stitches, formerly anathema to me, became so tempting that, in the end, I was seduced.

I can see you shaking your head, wondering how on earth I will be able to justify this complete about-face from the logical position I have until now been advocating. I can only explain that I developed, not long ago, a strong desire to own certain Chinese paintings, prints of which I had unearthed in my research in the field of oriental art. I wanted to hang these pictures on my walls. I wanted to enjoy them daily. These scrolls, however, belong to world-famous museums. Theft never crossed my mind. Being married to a judge, I above all must be a law-abiding person. Only a legal way to own these paintings would ever do. The answer became obvious: I must reproduce them myself, in one way or another, as well as I possibly could.

The thought of trying to make water-color copies on silk or paper filled me with horror—for, although I am a painter, I knew I could never achieve anything remotely like the subtle chiaroscuro and sure, fluid brush strokes that give the original works a good part of their unique charm. Furthermore, few things have ever struck me as being more hideous than inept copies of great works of art.

I never even considered a photographic print.

An oriental feeling for flat pattern and delicate shading is evident in the paintings I covet. An indigenous taste for the same qualities also moved the minds and hands of those needleworkers responsible for the countless tapestries produced, century after century, in China. How else can one account for the strong similarity between the paintings and embroideries of Far Eastern origin? The idea of translating "my" paintings into stitches worked in silk on canvas therefore came to me as a natural solution to my needs. What is more, even after consideration, I found that this particular method of reproducing my favorite scrolls did not at all offend my sense of artistic propriety.

To date my intention is to make four horizontal panels, one for each season so that I may tell what time of year it is without looking at the calendar. This may be my way of asking the tapestries to perform, for my puritanical heart's sake, a vague sort of function to justify their existence.

For my project I have chosen suitable materials. I am using #14 canvas because of the detail it allows. I am using silk for the stitching. The range of colors available to me offers a most opulent palette of over five hundred hues and tones. Silk is admittedly less sturdy than wool, but strength of fiber is, in this case, not a requirement, for each tapestry, when hung, will have to endure no wear more abrasive than the occasional glance sent across its surface.

No frames will surround my pictures except those I work in silk. And no glass will ever cover the panels, for each piece is

being worked as though it were a Chinese hand-scroll complete with embroidered mat and vertical wooden rods.

Other than the obvious differences of stitching and style, most tapestries bear a resemblance to each other. Mine, however, will be easily distinguished by the way in which they will hang: when mounted, they will span the long horizontal space between their two end rollers of wood. The traditional tapestry, usually vertical, has always hung simply from a single horizontal pole.

6

AT this point I would like to tell you about a few of the problems I have encountered when working out some of the designs in this book. In doing this I hope to be able to help you solve the occasional problems you may come up against when you create your own designs.

Considering the three areas again—the center, the field and the border—I find on examining my own designs that there is no hard and fast rule I follow as to the ratio of space I give to each part, for every design presents different problems, and each of these demands its own solution. It is simply a matter of giving the central motif enough breathing room in the field, then of scaling the width and detail of the border so it neither overwhelms the main design nor is overpowered by it. Balance and harmony are my goals. You must rely on your own sense of proportion when you place a border around a design.

When I designed the graphs for the Magpie, the Shrike and the Dove, I was using as my central motifs details from ancient Chinese masterpieces. Because a love of serene space is inherent in all these old paintings, I decided to use a very simple border, making it something like a Chinese moon-gate or window open-

Checkerboard

Circular Floral Pillow

Fish in Spiraling Waves

"Cracked Ice" Pillow

Serenity #2 Pillow

Sung Dynasty Dove

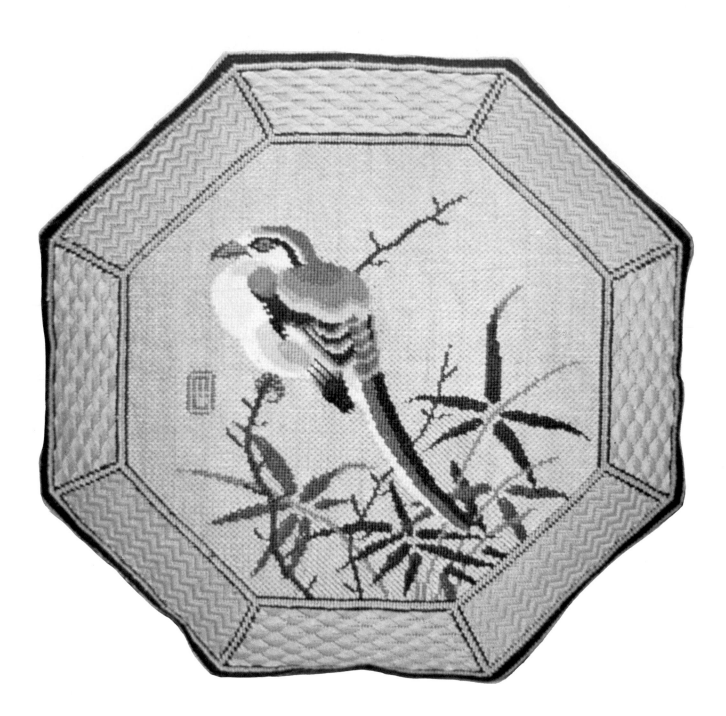

Shrike Pillow

Sung Magpie Pillow

Sung Dynasty Chinese painting "Magpie on a Viburnum Branch," THE
METROPOLITAN MUSEUM OF ART.

ing out on a scene of a bird on a branch. I felt that any change of tonal value between the field and the eight border panels would be distracting, so instead I used a change of texture. This seems to open the window wider, and so gives the picture even more breathing space.

When, on the other hand, a central motif is extremely complex, as it is in the Adam and Eve design, the antique Chinese floral plate pattern, or the fish in the spiraling waves, I let the design go almost to the edge of the area I will work. I then prefer to use a very simple, narrow border, reasoning that anything heavier would be too powerful and would detract from my center of interest. In this kind of design there is really no field: there is just pattern and border.

Designing the pillow with the pair of Sung Dynasty geese presented several problems. The birds, so simple and serene, charmed me completely from the moment I first saw them in a print of the old painting. But their basic outline lacked great interest, and could not instantly be recognized as a pair of birds. Furthermore, the detail within their outlines was so subtle that I felt I must create interest in the other two areas, the background and the border. So I fell back on the use of pattern.

Within the field I used a linear repeat motif to set off the curves of the geese; then in the border I turned to a free-flowing line that echoed the lines of the birds' bodies. I wanted the geese to remain the focal point in the design, so I subdued the tonal values of the border, and the key-fret background design was worked in very close tonal values. In this way neither background nor border would compete with the center of interest.

Incidentally, the little pale pink buds in the border illustrate a theory I have about the power of dots. To me they are visually very exciting. They always seem to dance on their backgrounds. Used unwisely they can be overwhelming. Used with discretion they can snap an otherwise dull design into something quite special.

7

On the following pages you may see designs that look forbidding and impossible to execute. Should this happen I have a suggestion to make: Remember that when you work you will be making only one stitch at a time, not all of them at once.

For fabric to match almost any color, send a sample of the color to:

> Mr. Lou Arnold
> Jerry Brown
> 85 Hester Street
> New York, New York 10002

For all "Au Ver à Soie" French silk numbers given in this book; for Medici wool numbers; and for Diane Tapestry wool numbers order from:

> C. R. Meissner and Co.
> 22 East 29th Street
> New York, New York 10016
> Attention: Miss M. Kuscher

This establishment will also fill orders for canvas when the order is for more than one yard.

D.M.C. cotton is available in almost every city in the United States. For further information write:

> The D.M.C. Corporation
> 107 Trumbull Street
> Elizabeth, New Jersey 07206

For most pillows 30 skeins of D.M.C. cotton are required for the background.

For most pillows 5 skeins of silk should cover the background. The silk floss comes in skeins. Each one is loosely bound, at the center, with a paper label on which appears a number. This wrapping—with glue on the inner side—is easily removed. Take it off, open up the skein, cut it once, where it is knotted, then re-wrap the paper label around the middle of the long, cut skein. This process is much like rolling a cigarette. Seal the label by moistening the free end. Do this so the number of the color is still visible. It is always advisable to keep your silk threads so numbered because some of the colors are very close and hard to distinguish from each other except by number—except when you have finished working the wrong color in a design!!!

How to clean wool needlepoint: Small pieces are easily cleaned. Buy a can of "Goddard's Spray Clean." Shake the can. Spray the entire piece of needlepoint thoroughly. The cleaning agent, a powder in a liquid vehicle, turns white when it dries. When the needlepoint is completely dry—about half an hour after spraying—brush off the white powder thoroughly. You may want to clean off the slightly sticky residue that clings to the wool surface. This can easily be done with a sponge dipped in a mild solution of ammonia and water. Wring the sponge out until it is only damp, then wipe the needlepoint until it is no longer sticky.

For needlepoint rugs, spot clean with cleaning fluid, then clean with Glamorene Dry-cleaner for Rugs. Then vacuum.

Note, important. Never iron work done with silk floss. Instead, tack the finished piece to a board, aligning edges of work to edges of board. Using a steam iron, held one inch above work, dampen work with steam. Let dry and then remove from board.

THE DESIGNS

NOTE: If the graphs in this book are too small for easy reading, you may want to have them photostated and enlarged. They will reproduce well. Several people told me they had followed this procedure with graphs in *Needlepoint by Design*. Also, a photostat of the design packs easily into your needlepoint work bag.

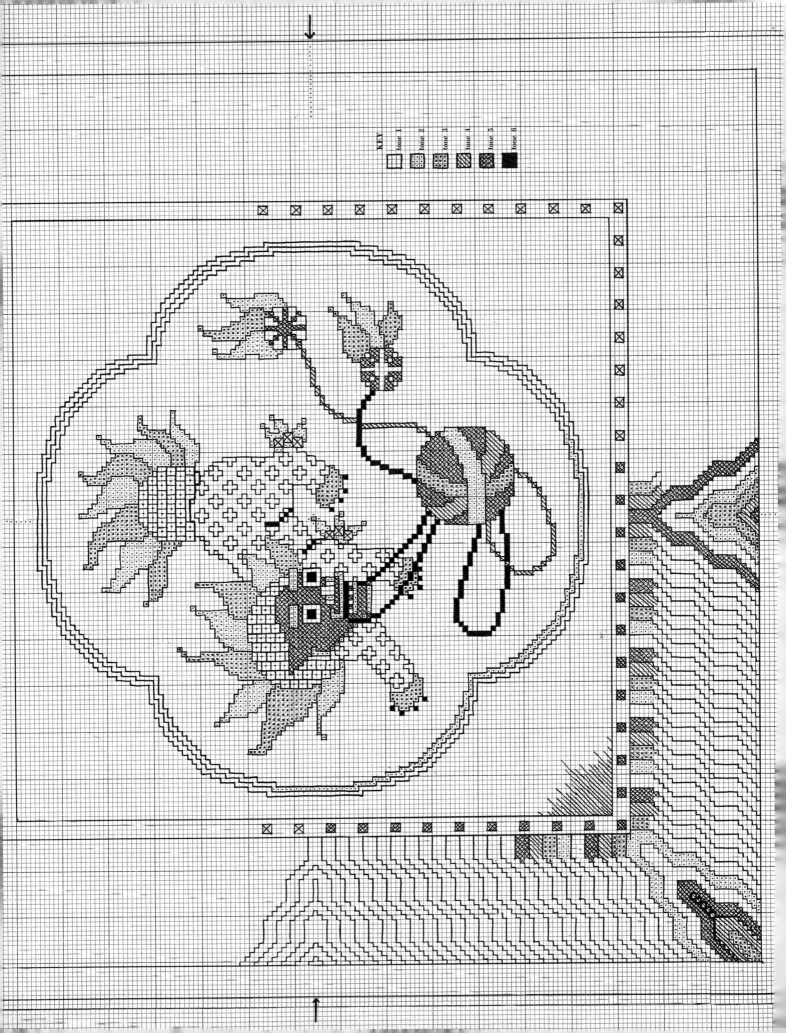

Foo Lion Pillow

17" x 17"

THE pillow measures 207 threads by 207 threads. Bind off a piece of #12 canvas measuring 21" x 21". Mark the two center threads, mark outlines, then draw graph lines in area where you will work Foo Lion.

A small, shaded square with four dots around it sits at the end of the upper flame on the lion's left front elbow. This square represents the center of the graph, and corresponds to the point on your canvas where the two center threads intersect. Use these two corresponding points for reference when you begin work. (When working the design, this stitch will be worked in #2 tone.)

Six tones are used in the design. They are:

1. Light or white
2. Medium light
3. Medium
4. Medium dark
5. Dark
6. Black

The original pillow was made with Persian wool. The key to the colors used follows:

1. 032 porcelain blue-white
2. 594· celadon green
3. 381 slate blue
4. 540 olive green
5. 721 royal navy blue
6. Black

1. Using #6 tone, black, work rope where it is black on graph.
2. Using #2 tone work upper and lower lip, eyebrows, 4 stitches in nose, and outline of jaw.
3. Using #1 tone outline eyes, work nose and teeth.

4. Using #6 tone work Smyrna cross stitches for eyes.
5. Using #5 tone fill in face.
6. Using #4 tone and Smyrna cross stitches, work mane around head. The rows of bumps are worked vertically in the mane, and horizontally in the tail. They are also staggered. Where there is NO box of 4 stitches—which symbol means work a cross stitch here—fill in with regular flat stitches.
7. Using #2 and #3 tones work flames around mane.
8. Using #4 tone work Smyrna cross stitches in tail.
9. Using #2 and #3 tones work flames around tail.
10. Using #3 tone work three visible feet, then make #6 toenails.
11. Using #4 tone work cross-shaped dots on lion's legs and body.
12. Using #5 tone fill in body.
13. Using #3 tone put in an overstitch dot in the center of each of the cross-shaped dots worked in step 11. By that I mean, work the center stitch only when a cross-shaped dot presents its center stitch for covering.
14. Using #2 tone work flames at elbow of front left leg, and behind rear left leg. Use Smyrna cross stitches for the X'd squares.
15. Using #4 tone work lighter part of rope, shaded on graph.
16. Using tones #2 through #5 work large ball of wool and two smaller tassels.
17. Using #2 tone work inner outline of clover shape.
18. Using #1 tone work outer outline of clover shape, then fill in background of clover area, i.e., all around the lion.
19. Using #5 tone and Smyrna cross stitches, work dots in border.
20. Using #1 tone work background of dotted band.
21. Using #4 tone and fatter yarn, i.e., three or four strands, work brick stitch between clover shape and dotted band. I work the stitch turned on its side. This way it LOOKS like bricks. You may of course prefer to use the regular basket weave stitch, in which case, go ahead with it.
22. Using tones #1 through #5 work zigzag border.

23. Using #1 tone work outer band, 5 rows wide.
24. Block and finish pillow.

In the event that you would like to make the Foo Lion pillow in D.M.C. cotton floss, follow the preceding instructions except for these changes: bind off a piece of #14 canvas measuring 19″ by 19″. The finished pillow will measure about 15″ by 15″. The cotton floss comes with six strands clinging together. Use nine.

The following colors are suggested:

1. 3072 white, or use blanc neige
2. 3053 sage green
3. 931 blue
4. 580 olive green
5. 820 royal blue
6. 310 black

In the event that you would like to make the Foo Lion pillow in French silk, use #14 canvas for a finished pillow that will measure about 15″ by 15″. The silk comes with seven strands clinging together. Use five.

The following colors are suggested:

1. 1741 off-white
2. 3722 sage green
3. 1433 blue
4. 514 olive green
5. 116 royal blue
6. noir, black

(Here, as elsewhere in the book, the names I give the colors are my own. The manufacturers do not name their colors. They only give them numbers.)

Cloud Band Pillow

16″ x 16″

THE face of the pillow measures 191 threads by 191 threads. Bind off a piece of #12 canvas measuring 20″ by 20″. Mark outlines and center threads. NOTE: Draw first two graph lines 4 threads to the right and left of vertical center thread, and the next two graph lines 4 threads above and below horizontal center threads. (Center panel of threads between graph lines will then be only 9 threads wide, to correspond to graph where center panels are only 9 box-stitches wide.) Finish marking face of pillow with graph lines 10 threads apart. In this way you can use the graphed quarter of the border for all four quarters of the pillow.

There are five tones in the Cloud Band pillow. Suggested Persian wool colors are:

1. 107 white
2. 396 pale blue
3. 386 medium blue
4. 034 tan
5. 334 dark blue

The graph has been drawn with tonal symbols in each square so no instructions are necessary for the placement of tones, *except* that the field within the cloud band, against which the central double happiness character and the four corner flower motifs are silhouetted, is worked in #4 tone. The outer band is worked in #1 tone.

With D.M.C. cotton floss and #14 mesh canvas you can make a finished pillow measuring 13½″ by 13½″. Cut your canvas 18″ by 18″.

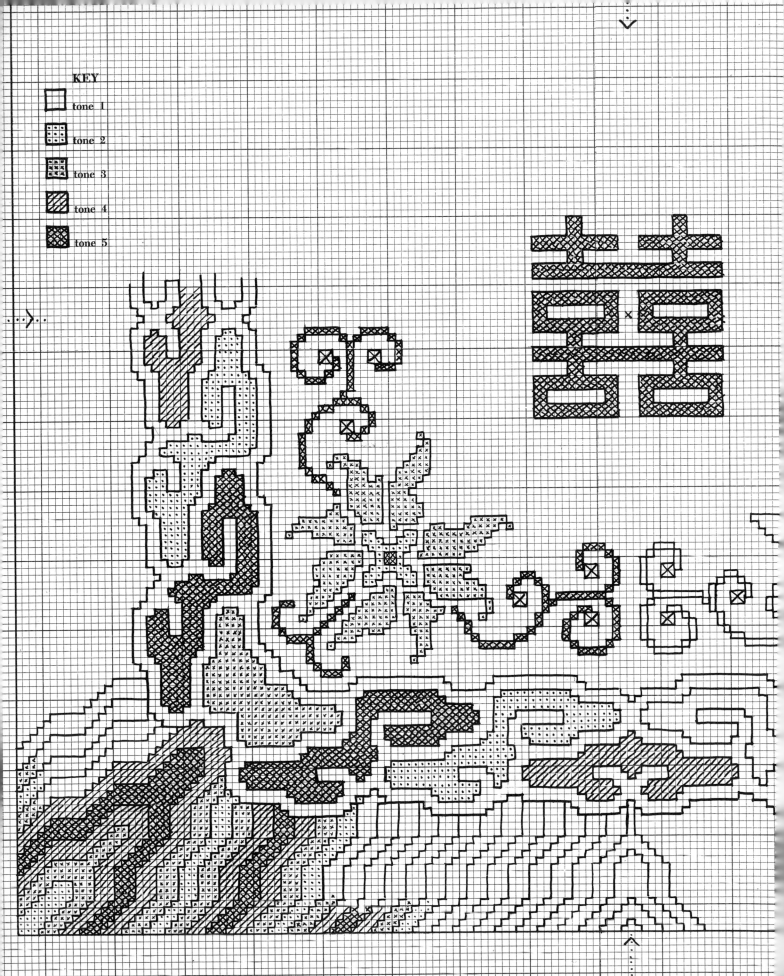

KEY

tone 1

tone 2

tone 3

tone 4

tone 5

Suggested D.M.C. colors follow:

1. 822 beige
2. 3325 light blue
3. 932 medium blue
4. 612 tan
5. 930 dark blue

With French silk and #14 mesh canvas you can make a finished pillow measuring 13½" by 13½". Cut your canvas 18" by 18".

Suggested French silk colors follow:

1. 3831 white
2. 1711 light blue
3. 1712 medium blue
4. 3833 tan
5. 1714 dark blue

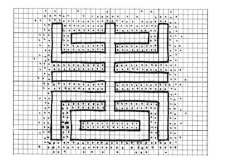

Adapted from an antique longevity symbol

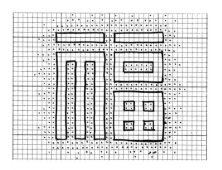

From Mother's Pewter Plate—Peking

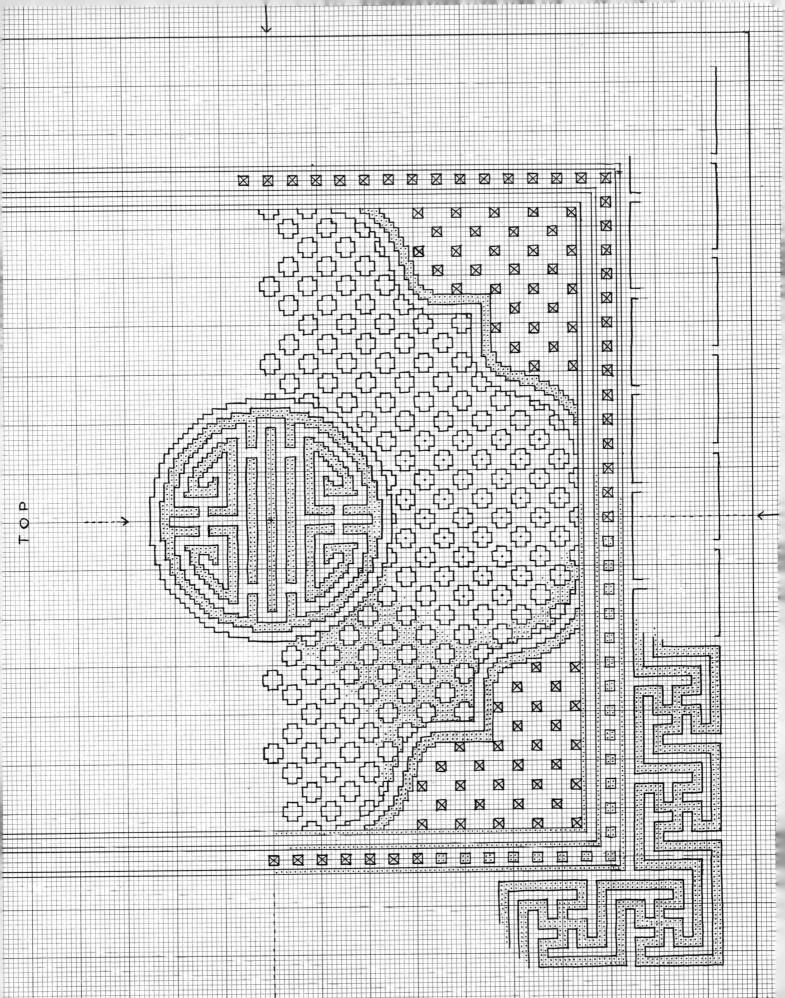

TOP

Serenity II Pillow

17" x 17"

THE pillow measures 200 threads by 200 threads. Bind off a piece of #12 canvas measuring 21" x 21". Mark vertical and horizontal center lines. Outline the pillow. Draw graph lines within the work area.

There are three tones in the design:

1. Light
2. Medium
3. Dark

Suggested colors in Persian wool:

1. 017 gray-white
2. 145 tobacco brown
3. 117 eggplant

1. Using #1 tone work central character and circle around it.
2. Using #2 tone fill in background around central character.
3. Using #3 tone work single inner row of bands outlining field.
4. Using #1 tone work white outer borders of bow-shaped corner pieces.
5. Using #3 tone work shaded inner borders of bow-shaped corner pieces.
6. Using #2 tone work eyelet stitch in field. See pp. 18, 27.
7. Using #3 tone fill in background around eyelets.
8. Using #2 tone work Smyrna cross stitches in bow-shaped corner pieces. Then fill in with #2 tone.
9. Using #3 tone work outlines of the band between the outer swastika border and the line outlining field. Smyrna cross stitches dot the band you are now outlining. These are also to be worked in #3 tone.
10. Using #2 tone fill in background of band you have just outlined and dotted in step 9.

11. Using #3 tone work swastikas.
12. Using #1 tone fill in remainder of pillow, i.e., between dotted band and outline of field, and behind swastikas out to the edge of the pillow.
13. Block and finish pillow.

Chinese Butterfly Design

Fluttering Ribbon Border

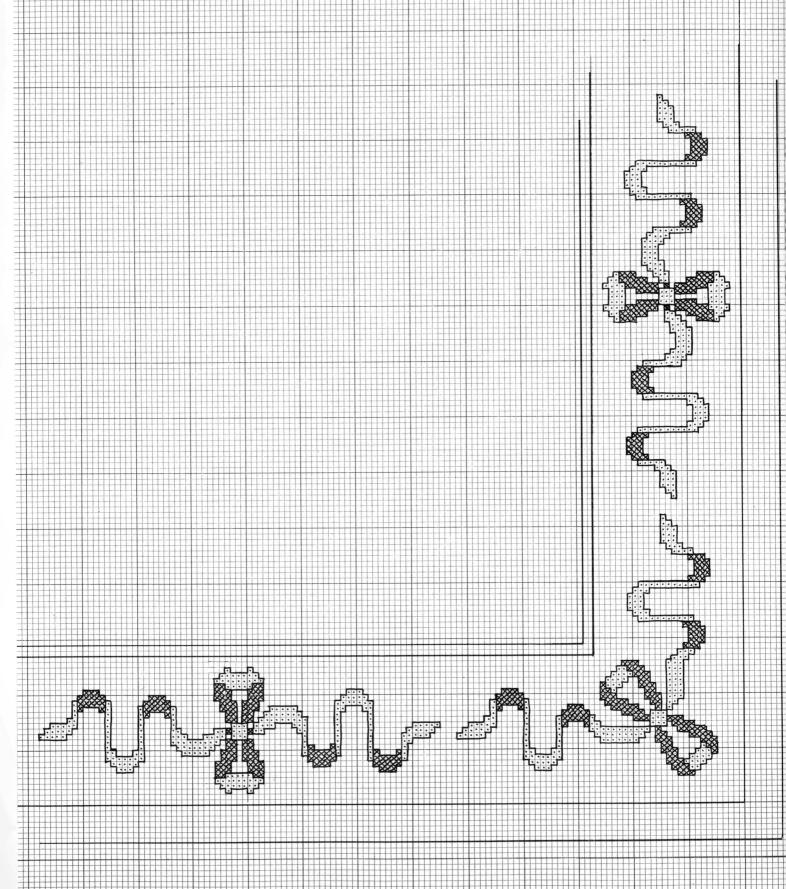

Flaming Pearl Pillow

16" x 16"

THE pillow measures 204 threads by 204 threads. Bind off a piece of #12 canvas measuring 20" x 20". Mark the two center lines, mark the four outlines, then draw graph lines in your work area.

Four tones are used in the Flaming Pearl pillow:

1. Light
2. Light medium
3. Medium
4. Dark

The original pillow was made with Persian wool. The key to the colors used follows:

1. 012 creamy white
2. 563 olive beige
3. 358 Chinese blue
4. 117 eggplant

In order to simplify a complex design and make work easier for you I have given you two graphs for this pillow. The first graph is of the flaming pearl motif. (An ╬ marks the center of both graphs and corresponds to the crossing of the two center lines on your canvas.) The second graph is of the background and border.

The graphs have been prepared with tonal symbols in each square so no instructions are necessary for tonal placement.

Outline the two circles and the flaming pearl in graph one, then fill in with the indicated colors.

Turn to graph two; outline the field, then work the overlapping shells in the field. Then work border.

In the event that you would like to make the Flaming Pearl in D.M.C. cotton floss, follow the preceding instructions except for these changes: bind off a piece of #14 canvas measuring 18" by 18". You will make a pillow about 14" by 14".

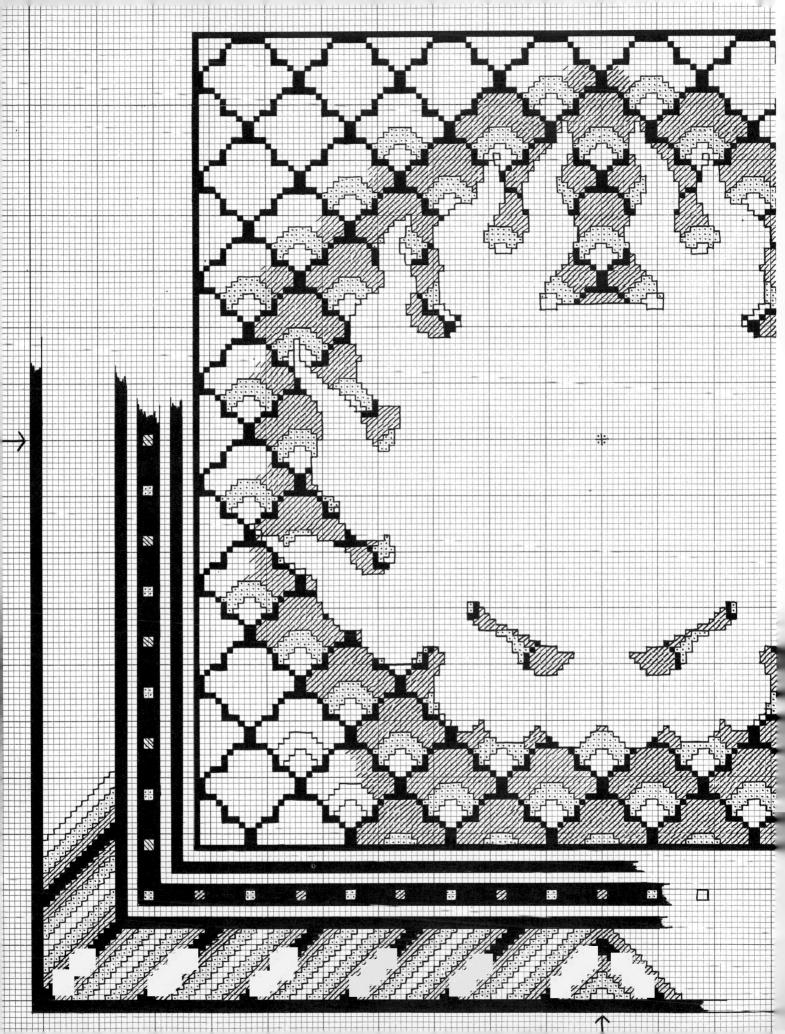

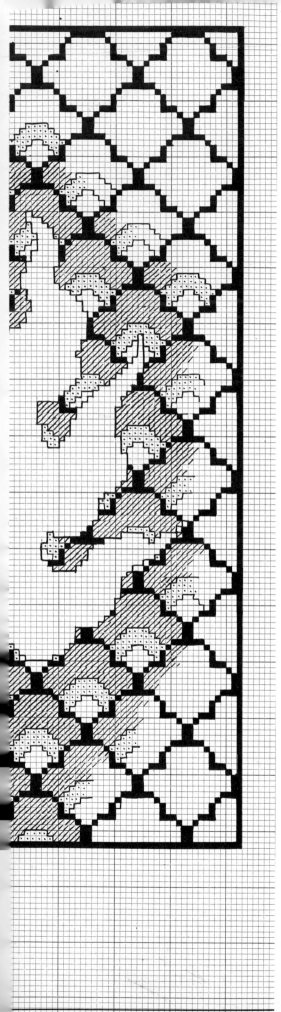

The cotton floss comes with six strands that cling together. Use nine.

The following colors are suggested:

1. 3072 off-white
2. 3013 pale avocado
3. 322 Chinese blue
4. 3051 dark avocado

In the event that you would like to make the Flaming Pearl in French silk, you also use #14 canvas for a finished pillow which will measure about 14″ by 14″.

The French silk comes with seven threads clinging together. On #14 canvas, use five.

The following colors are suggested:

1. 3711 off-white
2. 2133 pale avocado
3. 1724 Chinese blue
4. 3326 eggplant

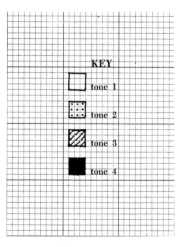

KEY

tone 1
tone 2
tone 3
tone 4

(77)

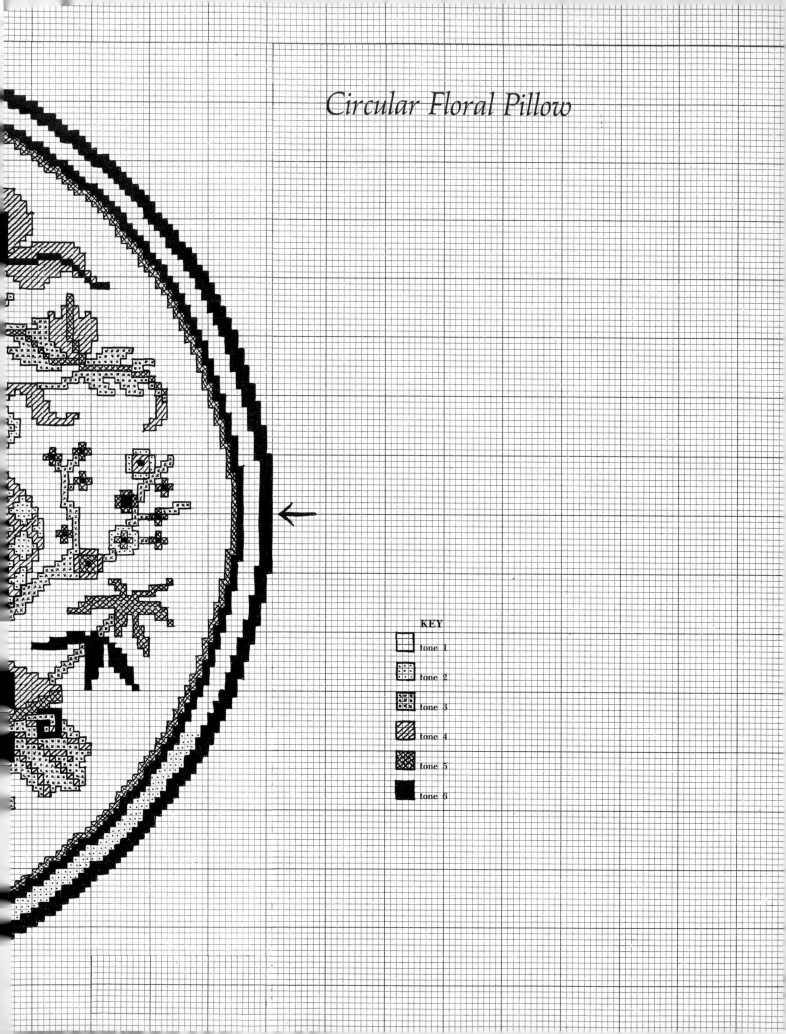

Circular Floral Pillow

KEY

☐	tone 1
⊡	tone 2
▥	tone 3
▨	tone 4
▩	tone 5
■	tone 6

Circular Floral Pillow

13¾" diameter with 2½" boxing

THE square within which the circle fits measures 162 by 162 threads. Bind off a piece of #12 canvas measuring 18" by 18". Mark horizontal and vertical center lines. Mark the outlines of the square. Mark the graph lines within the work area.

There are six tones in the design. They are:

1. White
2. Light
3. Light medium
4. Medium
5. Medium dark
6. Dark

The original pillow was made with Persian wool. The key to the colors used follows:

1. 005 white
2. 396 pale blue
3. 386 light medium blue
4. 385 medium blue
5. 330 medium dark blue
6. 365 navy blue

This design was taken from an antique Chinese plate recently found in the ash pile of an early colonial military encampment on the eastern coast of Canada. The plate had evidently been discarded because badly broken. When found, however, it was pieced together and photographed for an art magazine. There I saw it and felt that it would lend itself well to needlepoint. Since the design was originally created for porcelain, I think it should be worked in traditional glaze colors, such as olive, deep to pale, or eggplant, from dark to faded amethyst, for example.

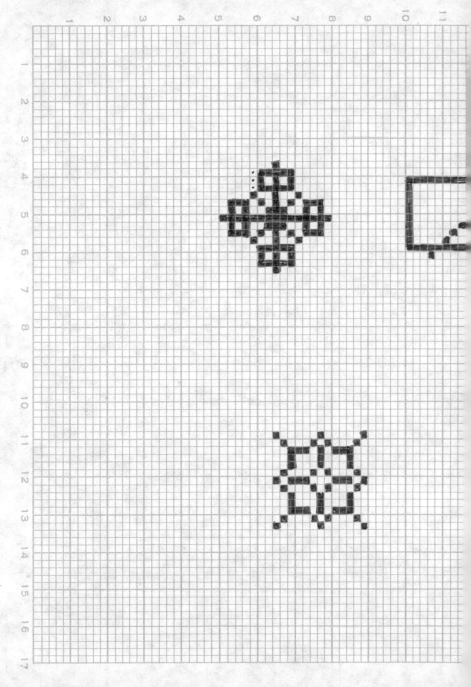

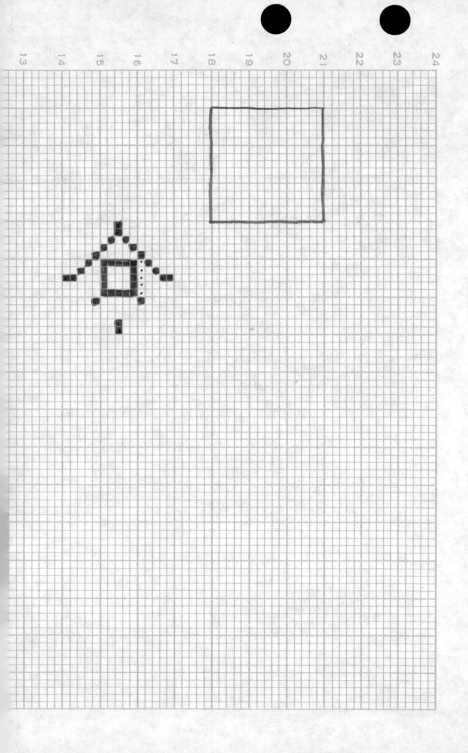

The graph has been drawn with tonal symbols in each square so no instructions are necessary for the placement of tones.

BOXING BAND

For the boxing band bind off a strip of canvas 55″ in length by 6″ in width. The working area measures 505 threads in length by 31 threads in width. Mark it off with graph lines in the areas where the panels will be worked. Each panel measures 45 threads from end to end and 25 threads from top to bottom. The panels are separated by areas measuring 56 threads in length. Place the panels on the strip as follows:

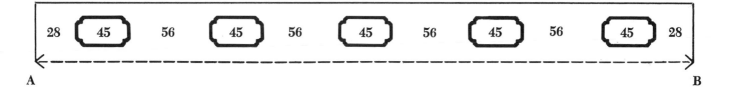

When you are ready to join the band to the face of the pillow you must first join the two ends together. Fold the panel in half with the inside out. Sew the two ends together by hand using #2 wool thread. For a neat seam, match the canvas threads of one end to the corresponding canvas threads of the other end. Press seam open. Pin the side of the band between A and B to the face of the pillow. I first mark three lines on the band: the center and half way from center to one end. These three lines match the

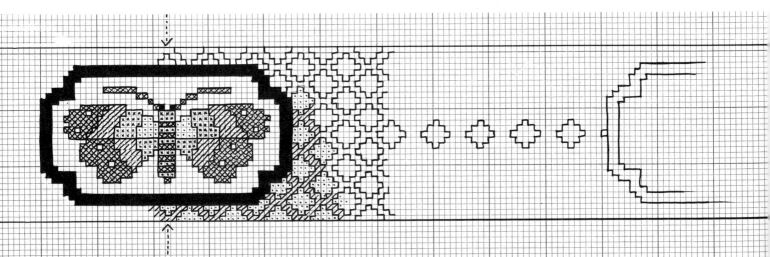

center top and the two side centers on the face of the pillow. The band seam, of course, goes to the bottom center. After pinning the band all the way around, sew the band to the face of the pillow by hand, using #2 wool thread. Do not catch in seam allowances of banding seam. Press round-the-pillow seam toward boxing.

For the back of the pillow cut a circle of silk and wool to match the #2 tone. Make it 1½″ larger in diameter than the face of the pillow. Use the sewing machine to baste, on the backing, the outline of a circle exactly matching the size of the face of the pillow. Put your custom made pillow inside the needlework band (already joined to face of pillow cover). Turn in raw edge of banding. Pin banding to backing along basting line. Slip stitch. Give a final touch up by pressing the pillow once with a damp cloth and a steam iron.

If you plan to make the Circular Floral pillow in D.M.C. cotton floss, follow the preceding directions, but use #14 canvas for a pillow which, when finished, will measure 11½″ in diameter with a boxing slightly deeper than 2″.

Suggested colors are:

1. 3072, or use blanc neige
2. 827 light blue
3. 813 medium light blue
4. 826 medium blue
5. 825 medium dark blue
6. 824 dark blue

Suggestions for French silk colors are:

	BLUES	GREENS	LAVENDERS
1.	73 blanc	73 blanc	73 blanc
2.	1711	1841	4631
3.	1712	1842	4632
4.	1713	1843	4634
5.	1714	1844	4645
6.	1716	1845	4646

Rosalia Alpina Longicorn Beetle

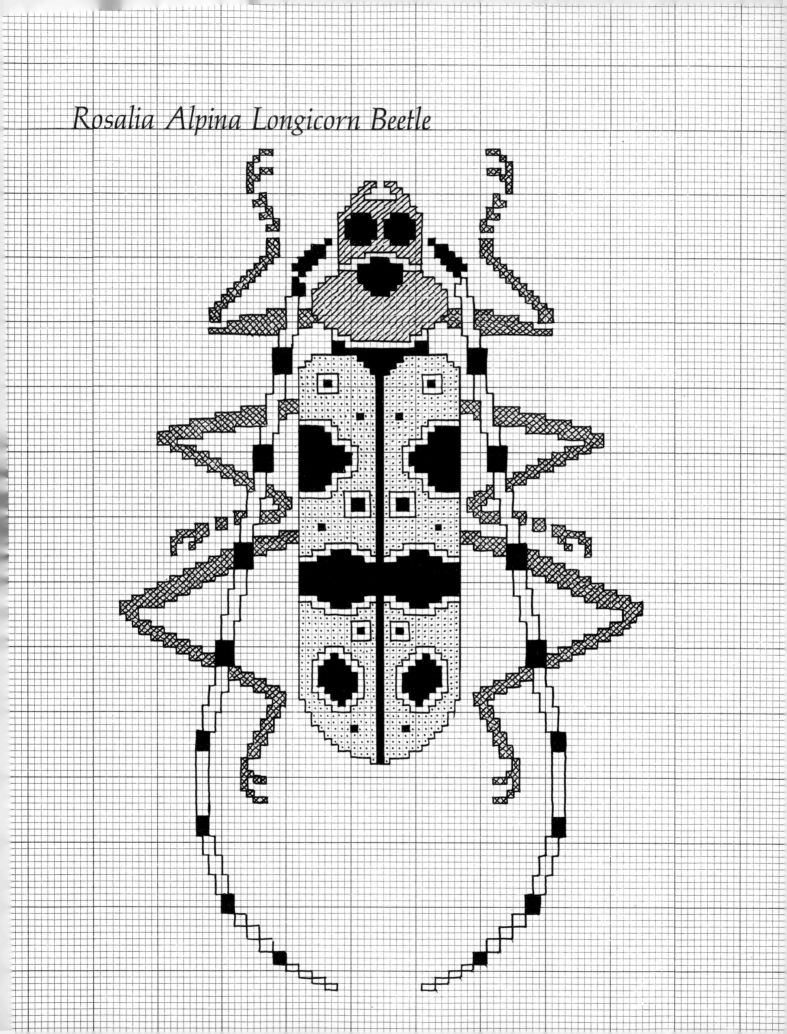

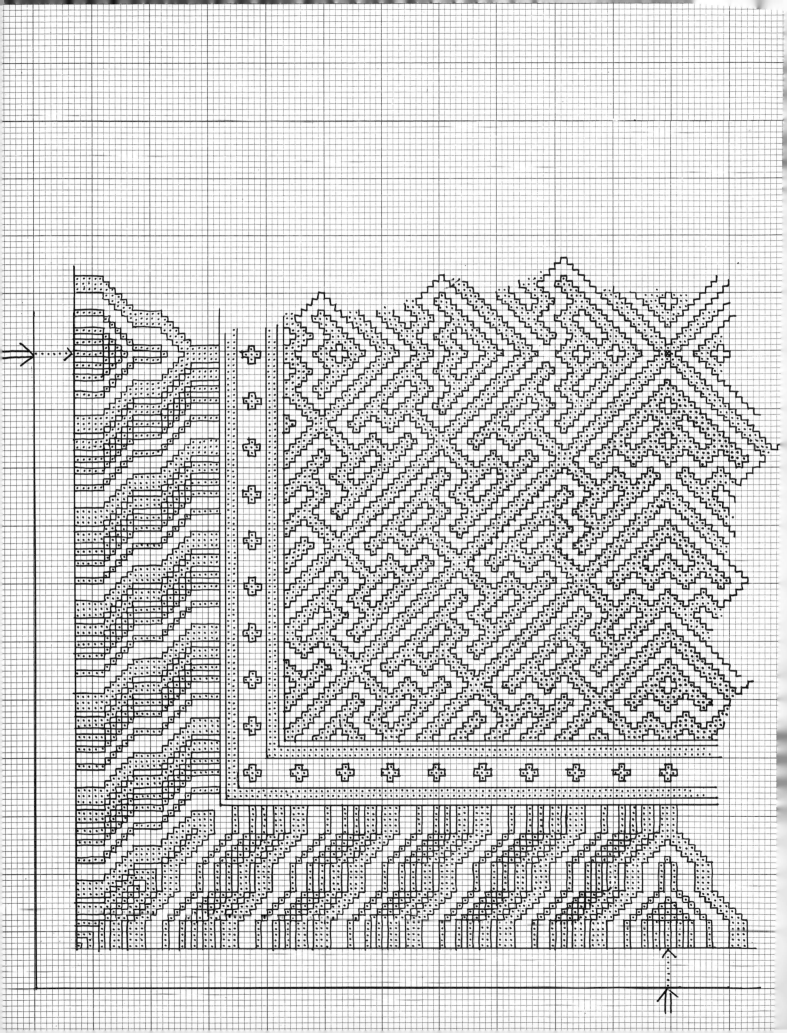

"Cracked Ice" Pillow

18" x 18"

THE pillow measures 219 threads by 219 threads. Bind off a piece of #12 canvas measuring 22" by 22". Mark the two center threads and the outlines of the pillow. Then mark the graph lines of the work area. NOTE: When marking the graph lines on your canvas, count off nine threads between the vertical center thread and the first graph lines to the left and right of it. Then count off nine threads between the horizontal center thread and the first graph lines above and below it. Finish marking canvas with graph lines ten threads apart. In this way you can use the graph for all four quarters of the pillow.

There are two tones in the design. They are light and dark. I used white and navy in the original pillow. You may of course use close harmony, that is, two tones close to each other in value, like tobacco brown and navy blue. You will still have an exciting pattern. SUGGESTION: The design may be reversed to produce an interesting companion pillow. That is, a light tone would then be used for the areas shaded on the graph, and a dark tone would be used for the areas left white on the graph.

A small, square area rug, 31" by 31", could be made from this graph using #7 Penelope canvas and 4 strands of Persian wool.

In the instructions for some of the following pillows, where many colors are used and step-by-step instructions would therefore become cumbersome, I have simply listed the colors by number, and indicated where they appear in the design. I list them in the order that I would use them, starting from the center of interest and working out.

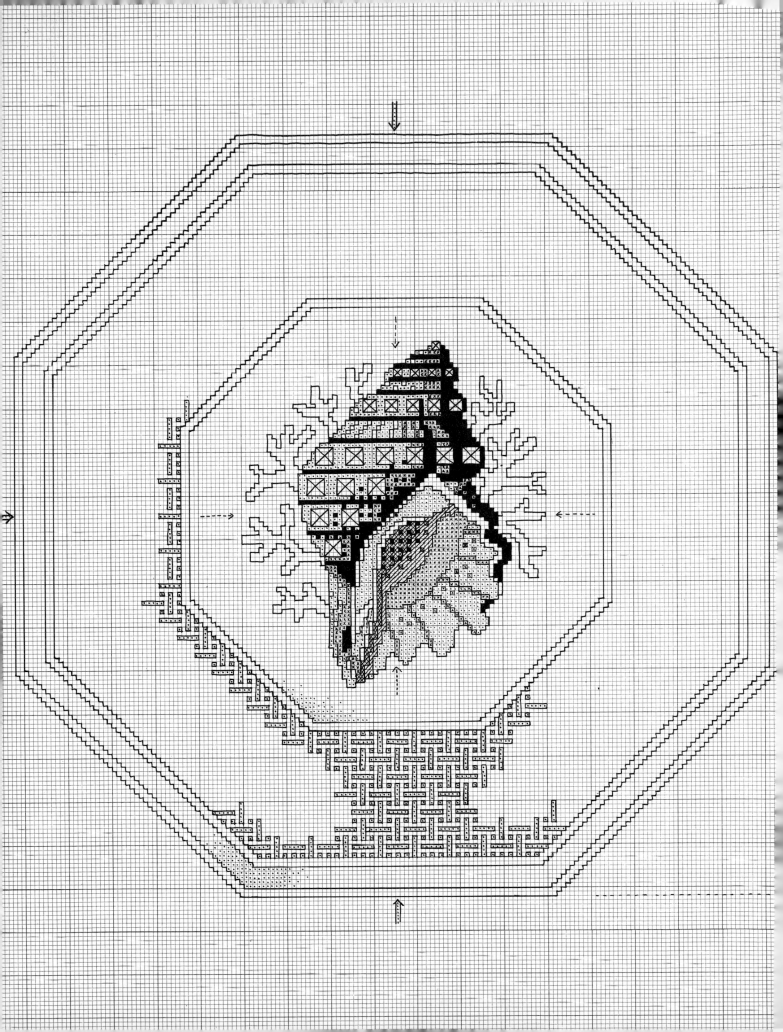

Shell Pillow

OCTAGON 14¼″ in diameter

THE square within which the face of the octagon pillow fits measures 175 threads by 175 threads. Bind off a piece of #12 canvas measuring 19″ by 19″. Mark horizontal and vertical center threads. Mark outlines of square. Then draw graph lines in work area.

The original pillow was made with Persian wool. The key to the numbered colors, as used, follows:

1. Pure white — Use for lumps and white parts of outer shell, and for outlining octagon, in patterned area, and border.
2. 105 off-black — Use for black areas of outer shell.
3. 025 taupe — Use for darker parts of outer shell, with small x in shading.
4. 166 gray-beige — Use for light parts of outer shell, dotted on graph.
5. 464 pale orange — Use for inner shell, wherever it is dotted on graph.
6. 436 pale apricot — Use for second tone in inner shell.
7. 278 coral — Use for third tone in inner shell.
8. 225 deep coral — Use for fourth tone in inner shell, for background around shell, for patterned area around inner octagon, and for part of outer border.
9. 267 dark coral — Use for fifth tone in inner shell.
10. 426 apricot — Use for coral branches.

Work white bumps on outer shell. Use double Leviathan, triple cross, and Smyrna cross stitches. Then work the white dots and lines on outer shell, and the white line separating the inner from the outer shell, i.e., where the lip curls outward.

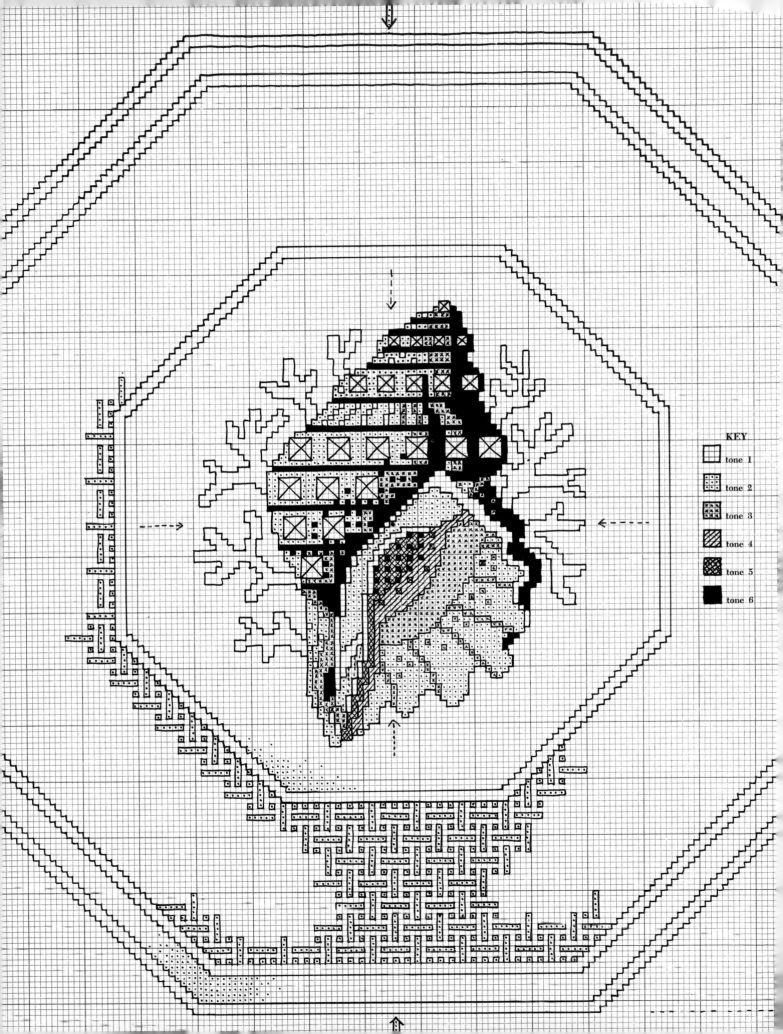

KEY

tone 1
tone 2
tone 3
tone 4
tone 5
tone 6

Work the black areas, the shaded areas, and the lighter parts of the outer shell.

Using five tones for the inner shell, shade it as marked on the graph.

Work the coral branches.

Work outlines of octagon around shell.

Fill in coral background around shell.

Work two outer outlines in white.

Work coral pattern in patterned area around shell octagon. Fill in white background of patterned area. Work coral area between two outer outlines.

The pillow requires a 2″ fabric boxing. (A knife edge on a circular or octagon pillow does not make up well.) Match your fabric to whatever color you have selected to use as the main color in the design; in the given instructions, the coral used around the shell and in the patterned area and border is the color to match. Cut a strip 52″ in length and 3½″ in width. For complete instruction on applying boxing bands and backing turn to p. 122.

GRAPH 1

Fish in Spiraling Waves

Adapted for needlepoint from Ching Dynasty porcelain plate. WORCESTER ART MUSEUM. MASS.

CIRCULAR, 14½″ in diameter

THE square within which the circle fits measures 170 threads by 170 threads. Bind off a piece of #12 canvas measuring 19″ x 19″. Mark center lines. Outline square. Draw graph lines in work area.

The original pillow was made in Diana Tapestry wool and D.M.C. cotton. Key to the colors used follows:

Diana Tapestry wool	3515	ice-blue
Diana Tapestry wool	5009	navy
D.M.C. cotton	832	dark gold
D.M.C. cotton	3047	light gold
D.M.C. cotton	928	ice-blue

The graph is very complex, so I have given you three separations: one graph for the ice-blue, heavy wave lines and for the curling, foaming wavelets; one graph for the fish and the dark outlines for the waves, i.e., outer and inner side of the curve around the ice-blue, heavy wave lines to be worked from graph one (NOTE: The dark line on the inner side of each wave is heavier than the dark line on the outer side of each wave because the inner line has an overlap stitch in each step in the curve); and one final graph for the alternating light and dark curving water lines within each wave.

GRAPH 1

Using 3515 ice-blue wool, work heavy wave lines starting in the center and working out. Work the eight curling, foaming wavelets. Use 3072 ice-blue cotton for the Smyrna cross stitches at the end of each tendril of foam.

GRAPH 2

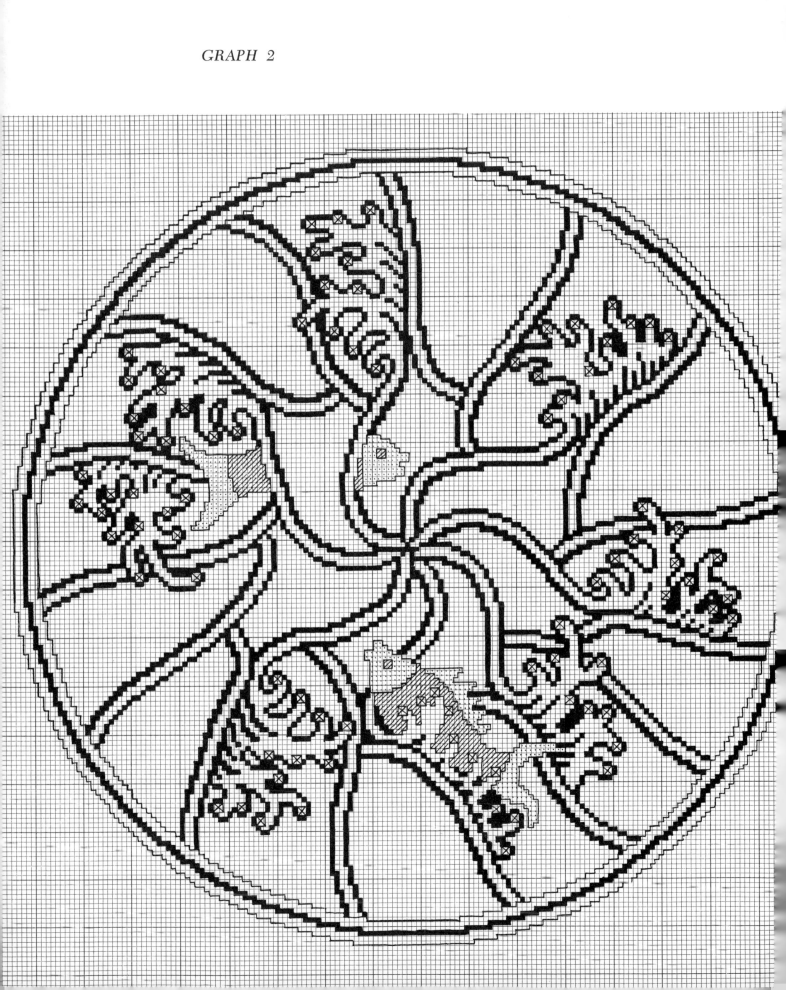

GRAPH 2

Work fish. Their bodies are 832 dark gold cotton, their heads, fins and tails are 3047 light gold cotton. You can, if you like, use a stitch like the Moorish stitch for working the bodies.

Work the outer border band around the pillow, using 3515 ice-blue wool and 5009 navy wool. Work outlines on inner and outer sides of heavy wave lines. Work from center out, reaching into and around the curls of foam.

GRAPH 3 (see page 94)

Using 3515 ice-blue wool and 5009 navy wool, work the light and dark curving water lines in each wave.

The pillow requires a 1½″ fabric boxing. Match it to the 5009 navy blue wool. Cut a strip about 50″ in length and 3″ in width. For complete instructions for applying boxing bands and backing, turn to p. 81.

If you want to make the pillow entirely in D.M.C. cotton, the following colors are suggested:

3072 ice-blue for bumps on waves.
 928 ice-blue for heavy wave lines, foam, and light water lines in each wave.
 336 dark blue for wave outlines and dark water lines in each wave.
 832 goldfish bodies.
3047 light gold fins, heads, and tails.

      or:

 747 aquamarine bumps, waves, foam, and light water lines in each wave.
3347 green for outlining heavy wave lines, foam and for dark water lines in each wave.
3042 mauve fish bodies.
 819 pale shell-pink fins, heads, and tails.

GRAPH 3

Lobster Design

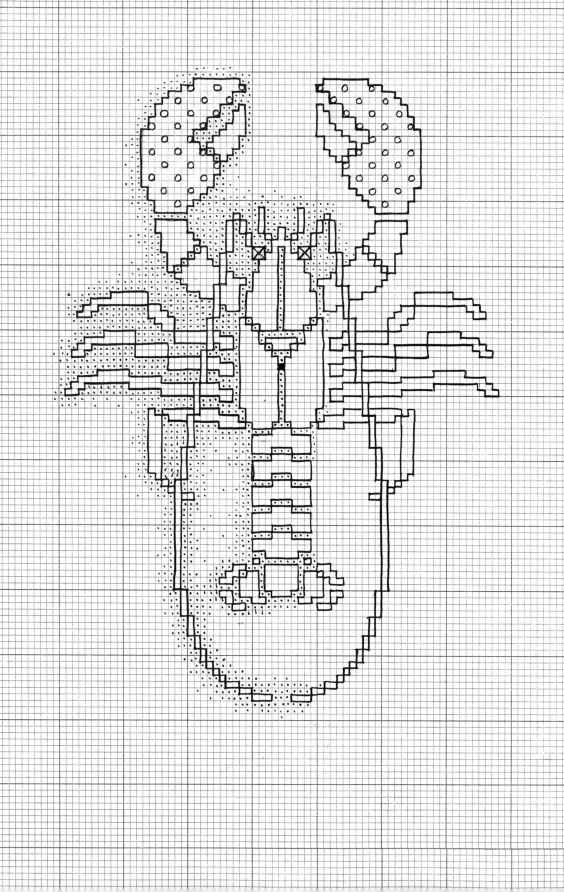

Island Temple
Scenic Pillow

PANEL B

*Island Temple
Scenic Pillow
Mirror Image*

Island Temple Scenic Pillow

12″ x 15½″ x 2½″ boxing

THE pillow measures 141 threads by 187 threads. Bind off a piece of #12 canvas 16″ by 20″. Mark center threads, mark four outlines, then draw graph lines in the work area.

Six tones are used in the Island Temple Scenic. They are:

1. White
2. Light
3. Light medium
4. Medium
5. Medium dark
6. Dark

The original pillow was made with Persian wool. The key to the colors used follows:

1. 017 off-white
2. 386 light blue
3. 385 light medium blue
4. 330 medium blue
5. 334 medium dark blue
6. 365 navy blue

This design was adapted from the decoration on an antique oriental Lowestoft porcelain mug in my possession. The piece is in blue and white with the delightful texture of an "orange-peel" glaze. It sits on my desk and holds my pens and pencils. One day I picked it up and, for the first time, looked at it intently. The wealth of detail it revealed excited me, and I immediately sat down to graph its design for needlepoint.

When I had finished the scene for the face of the pillow, I felt that it needed needlepoint boxing. So I searched through my oriental lacquer books until I found the appropriate design,

a case with rounded corners and floral panels. I adapted these to suit my pillow pattern, and soon I began my needlework.

I was so pleased by the resulting pillow that I made a mirror image of it, with one small change: a sailboat takes the place of one of the small islands of rocks in the original. At a later date I even augmented the design further, giving it a border so I could use it as a graph for an area rug worked on #7 Penelope canvas.

Since the original design was taken from a porcelain piece I like to think of it in antique glaze-like colors, worked in tones of blues, or greens, or lavenders, or perhaps even ranging from deep coral to faint bittersweet.

I have prepared the graph with tonal symbols in each box-stitch so no instructions are necessary for the placement of tones.

THE BOXING BAND

The work area in the band measures about 53″ in length and 2½″ in width. Bind off a piece of #12 canvas 58″ in length and 6″ in width. Count off an area 620 threads in length by 31 threads in width. The floral panels will be placed on it as follows:

| 81 | 15 | 117 | 15 | 163 |

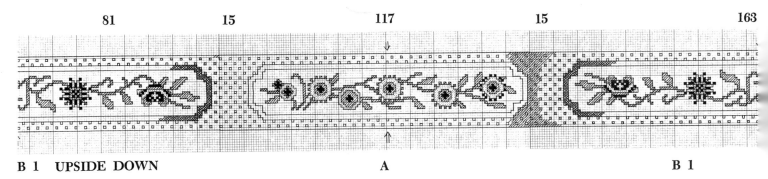

B 1   UPSIDE DOWN   A   B 1

After outlining the panel areas, mark the graph lines in each one. Again, the graph has been drawn with tonal symbols in the squares so no instructions are necessary for the placement of tones.

PUTTING THE PILLOW TOGETHER

Before you sew the boxing to the face of the pillow, take a piece of brown wrapping paper and draw on it the exact shape and size of the pillow's worked area. (Here I refer only to the face of the pillow.) Cut the paper to this size. Use it when you prepare the backing for the pillow. Place the paper pattern on the heavy, off-white silk and wool fabric you have chosen to match the off-white in the pillow's background. Use a pale gray coloring pencil and, on the fabric, draw a line around the paper pattern. Then, using the sewing machine, sew a line of off-white basting stitches along this gray line. With the same pencil, lightly mark the center lines on the top, the bottom, the two sides, and the four rounded corners of the backing. Allowing a ⅝″ seam allowance, cut around the row of basting stitches.

Now, sew the two ends of the banding together. Do it by hand, using #4 tone wool. Be sure to match the pattern at one end to the pattern at the other end of the banding. Press seam open. (The seam allowances on this seam will NOT be caught in the seam that joins the banding to the face of the pillow.)

Placing seam at bottom center, pin X to Y side of banding to face of pillow. Matching center lines at top, at sides, at four

| 15 | 117 | 15 | 82 |

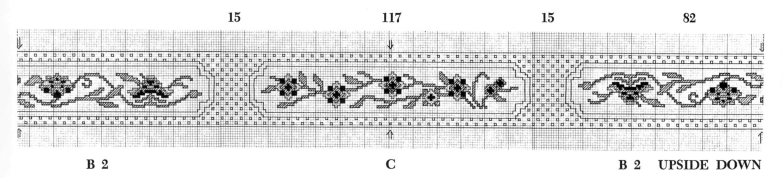

| B 2 | C | B 2 | UPSIDE DOWN |

corners, and of course at bottom, sew seam by hand using #1 tone wool. (Do not catch in seam allowance of banding while sewing the around-the-pillow seam.) Press seam toward boxing. Turn right side out.

Place custom-made pillow in pillow case. Turn under raw edge of boxing band. It will meet the basting line on the backing. Put backing in place on back of pillow and pin boxing band to basted seam line, matching the eight center marks, i.e., four sides and four corner centers. Slip stitch together. Steam and press all seams again.

Suggestions for making the Island Temple Scenic pillow in D.M.C. cotton follow:

Bind off a piece of #14 canvas measuring 14″ by 17″. Bind off a strip of #14 canvas measuring 50″ in length and 6″ in width. (Finished pillow will measure about 10″ x 13″ x 2″.)

Two possible sets of colors follow:

I	II
Tone #1 822 off-white	3072 porcelain white
Tone #2 3013 light olive	3325 light blue
Tone #3 3012 medium olive	334 light medium blue
Tone #4 3011 olive	332 medium blue
Tone #5 935 green	312 dark medium blue
Tone #6 823 navy	311 navy blue

Island Temple Scenic Rug

33″ x 59″

THE rug measures 221 double threads by 401 double threads. Bind off the ends of a piece of #7 Penelope canvas two yards long. It comes in 36″ widths so you do not need to bind the sides. They have selvages.

Mark center lines, horizontally and vertically. Mark outlines. Draw graph lines in the work area.

Six tones are used in the rug. They number from 1 to 6 as they number in the Island Temple pillow.

Use 4 strands of Persian wool when working the rug.

Use the following diagram to help you when working the pattern:

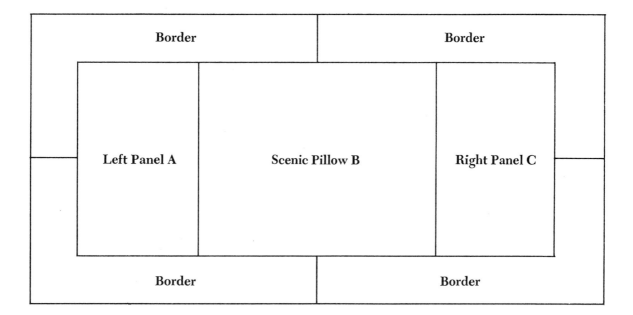

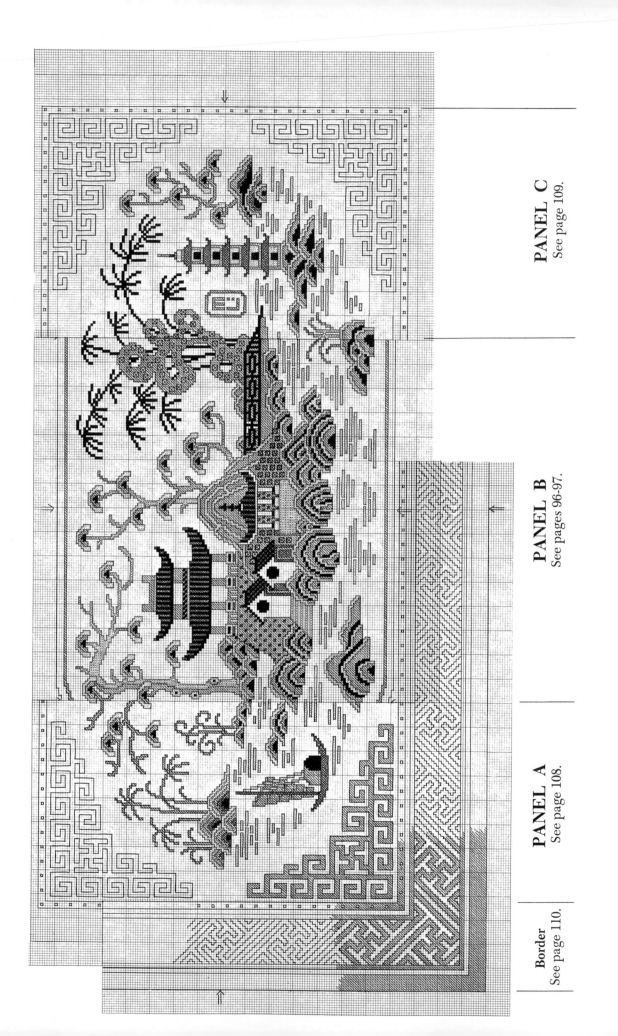

PANEL C
See page 109.

PANEL B
See pages 96-97.

PANEL A
See page 108.

Border
See page 110.

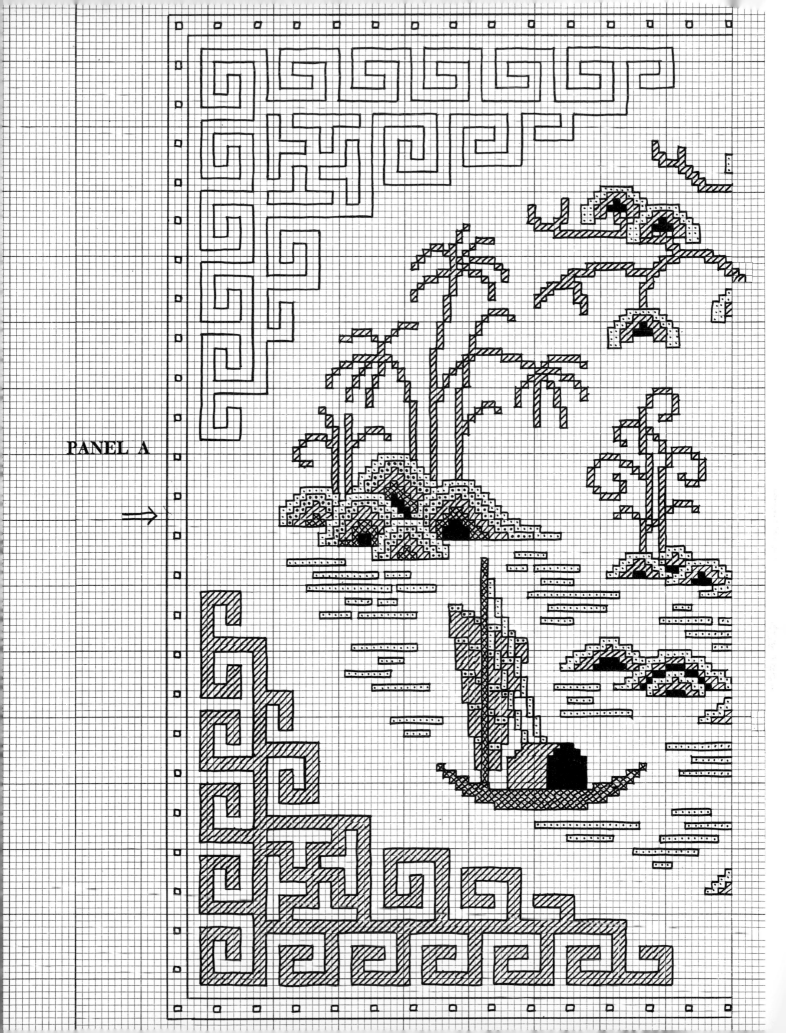

PANEL A

PANEL C

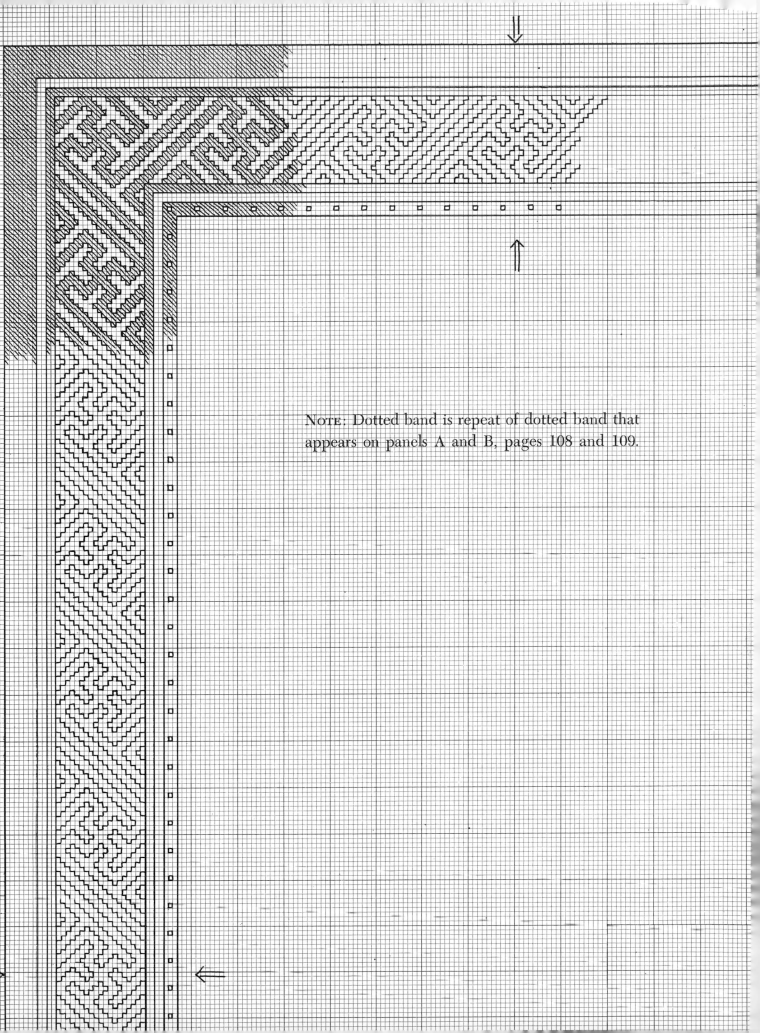

NOTE: Dotted band is repeat of dotted band that appears on panels A and B, pages 108 and 109.

Peony Rug

2 feet by 4½ feet

THE rug measures 176 threads by 380 threads. (It will be made on #7 Penelope canvas on which a double thread counts as a single thread.) Bind off a piece of #7 Penelope canvas measuring 2½′ by 5′. Mark horizontal and vertical center lines. Outline the rug, then draw graph lines in work area.

Use Persian wool for making the rug. Use four strands for adequate coverage, i.e., use the thread as it comes, three strands clinging together, and add a fourth strand.

The following tones and colors of Persian wool are suggested:

   #1 tone 017 off-white
   #2 tone 386 light blue
   #3 tone 385 medium blue
   #4 tone 330 medium dark blue
   #5 tone 365 navy blue

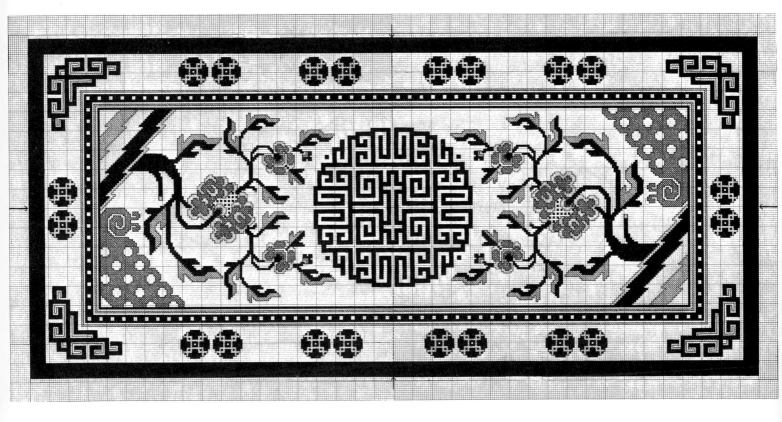

KEY

tone 1
tone 2
tone 3
tone 4
tone 5

Chinese Silkworm Moth Pillow

(Bombyx Mori, raised for silk in Asia since 2600 B.C.)

11" x 14" with 2" boxing

THE face of the pillow measures 145 threads by 193 threads. The boxing flaps measure 27 threads in depth. Bind off a piece of #14 mesh canvas measuring 19" x 22". Mark horizontal and vertical center threads. Outline pillow and pillow flaps. Draw graph lines in work area, i.e., for moth and frame around moth.

The original pillow was made with Medici wool and D.M.C. cotton. The key to the colors used follows:

Medici wool	401	lime green	
D.M.C. cotton	712	light ivory	tone #1
	822	beige	tone #2
	644	light tan	tone #3
	642	medium tan	tone #4
	640	dark tan	tone #5
	3031	brown	tone #6

1. Work the moth in the D.M.C. cotton colors, keyed on the graph with tonal symbols.

2. Work the frame for the field around the moth. Use #2 tone, #822 D.M.C. cotton.

3. Fill in background around moth, using #401 lime green wool. Using same color, outline frame worked in step 2. Outline face of pillow and four boxing panels. NOTE: Work all four flaps with stitches slanting at right angles to stitches on face of pillow.

4. Using #401 lime green wool and #822 beige cotton, work patterned area around moth panel, and on side flaps. NOTE AGAIN: Work all four flaps with stitches slanting at right angles to stitches on face of pillow.

5. Sew four corner seams by hand using #401 lime green wool.

6. Fill with pillow and sew lime green backing on the back of the pillow. Sew by hand, using slip stitch. Steam and press.

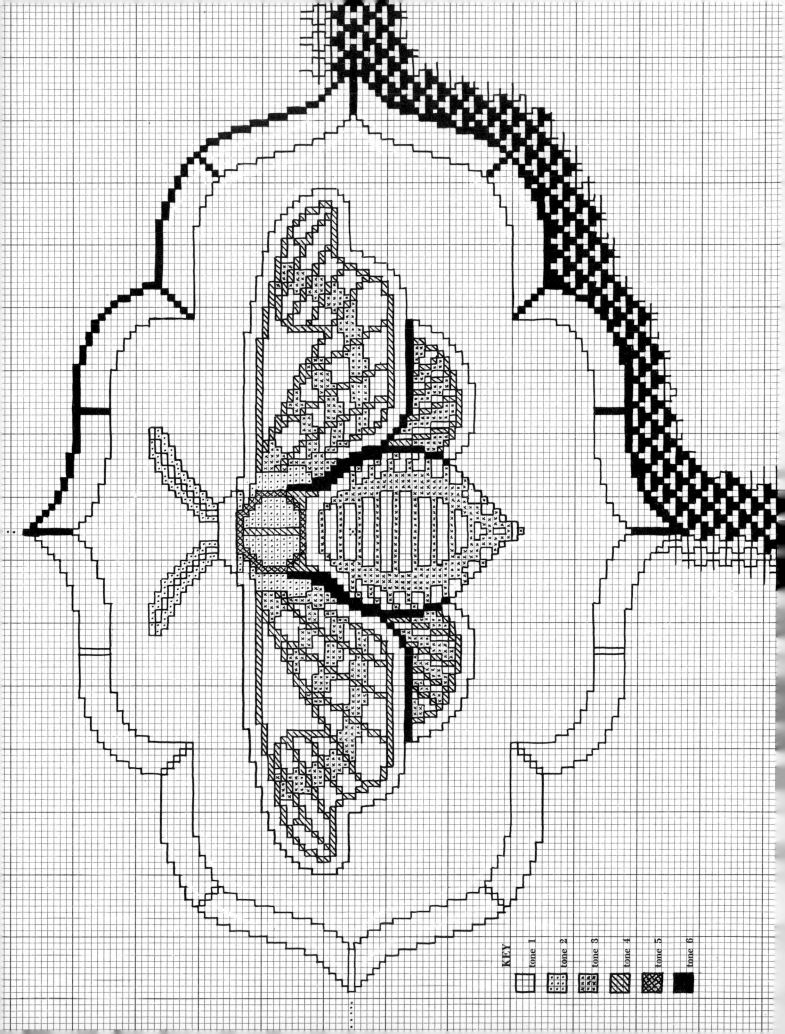

KEY

tone 1 tone 2 tone 3 tone 4 tone 5 tone 6

A Pair of Geese

From a Sung Dynasty painting, 960–1287 A.D., ARTIST UNKNOWN.

15½″ x 15½″

THE square within which the octagon fits measures 210 threads by 210 threads. Bind off a piece of #14 canvas measuring 20″ by 20″. Mark horizontal and vertical center lines. Mark outlines of square. Draw graph lines in work area.

The graph is quite complex so I have given you two separate graphs: one for the two geese and one for the rest of the pillow.

The original pillow was made with Medici wool, French silk and D.M.C. cotton.† Key to colors and materials used follows:

GRAPH 1 (see page 118)

Goose in foreground:

Black areas	Noir	Medici wool	black
White	Blanc	French silk	white
Dotted area	3711	French silk	off-white
Beak	105	Medici wool	apricot
Dark line in beak	104	Medici wool	russet
Shading under wing	3714	French silk	dark gray
	3713	French silk	medium gray
	3712	French silk	light gray
Eye	783	D.M.C. cotton	yellow

Goose in background:

Eye	783	* D.M.C. cotton	yellow
Beak	105	* Medici wool	apricot
Nostrils	104	* Medici wool	russet
Body	3712	* French silk	light gray
Dark lines in body	3713	* French silk	medium gray

* Signifies that the color has already been mentioned.
† For a pillow made entirely of D.M.C. cotton, see page 123.

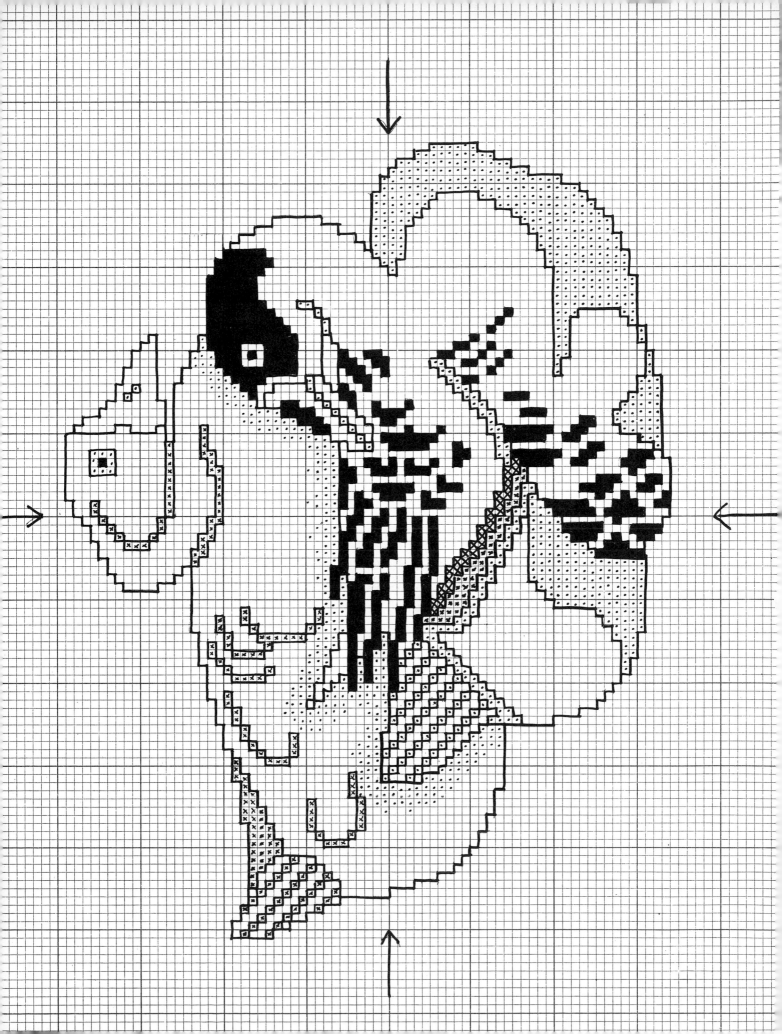

GRAPH 2 (see page 120)

Field:

Key fret	402	Medici wool	jade green
Background	309	Medici wool	olive brown

Outer panels:

Flowers in panels:	101 bis	Medici wool	palest coral
	109	Medici wool	light coral
	105	* Medici wool	coral
	104	* Medici wool	russet
Leaves in panels:	402	* Medici wool	jade green
Backgrounds of panels	309	* Medici wool	olive brown
Outline of panels			
and of pillow:	3712	* French silk	light gray

Box the pillow with a boxing 2″ in depth. Cut a piece of heavy silk, or silk and wool, to match the background color, in this case the olive brown. Cut the strip 60″ in length and 3½″ in width. The strip will end up only about 56″ in length, but it is best to allow a little extra length for the seam, which will be at the bottom of the pillow.

Allowing for seam, pin boxing band from Z, center bottom, to corner A. Sew from Z to A. (Sew this and all following seams with the needlepoint [wrong side of it] side up. Sew the seams as close as you can to the edge of the finished work.) Stop. Clip seam allowance of boxing band to corner, point A. Pin boxing band to pillow from corner A to corner B. Sew. Clip seam allowance of boxing band to corner B. Continue in same fashion all the way around the pillow until you get back to Z. Open up an inch or two on each side of this point. Join the two ends of the boxing band together and stitch. Press the seam open. Sew final seam between H and A, catching in boxing band seam and seam allowances at Z. Press the around-the-pillow seam open.

To make the octagonal backing, first take a piece of brown

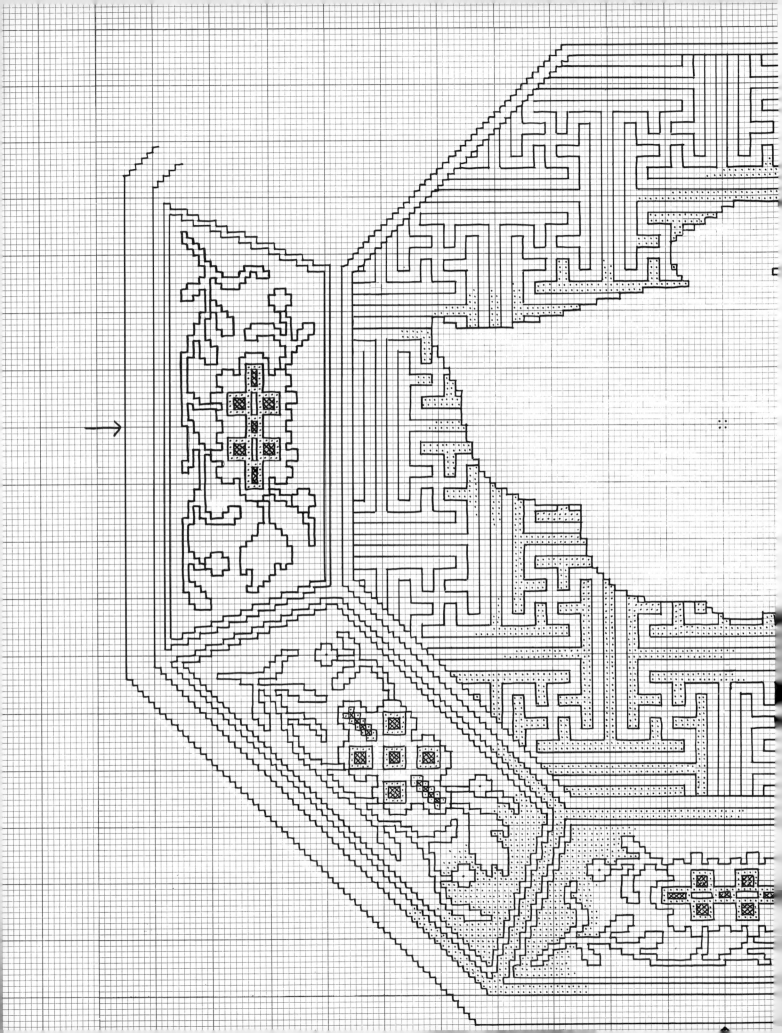

wrapping paper and draw on it the exact size and shape of the face of the octagon pillow, i.e., the entire worked area. Cut the paper to this size. Place the paper pattern on the fabric you have chosen for boxing band and backing. Use a tinted drawing pencil or a white sewing marker and, on the fabric, draw a line around the paper pattern. Then, using the sewing machine set for basting, sew a single line of long stitches, same color as fabric, along this line. Then cut the fabric around the basting line, leaving a ⅝″ seam allowance.

Turn under ⅝″ seam allowance on boxing band. Place custom-made pillow in boxed half of pillow covering. Pin boxing band to basted seam line on backing, matching eight corners. Slip-stitch together. Steam and press all seams again.

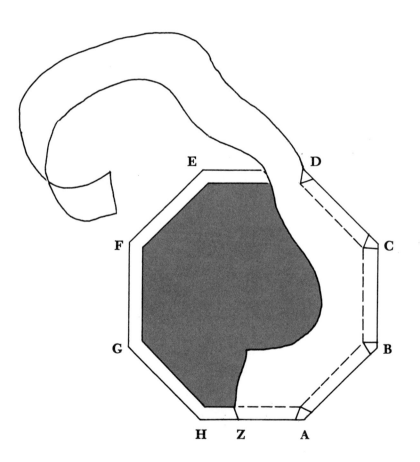

D.M.C. cotton floss colors for Pair of Geese pillow:

GRAPH 1

First goose:

Black	310	
White	Blanc neige	
Off-white	822	
Shading under wing	646 dark	
	2023 medium	
	644 light	
Beak	3064	
Dark line in beak	632	
Eyes	783 and 310	

Second goose:

Body	644
Lines in body	3023
Eyes	783 and 310
Beak	3064
Nostrils	632

GRAPH 2

Field:

Key fret	580
Background	935

Border:

Outlines of panels	822
Outline of pillow	822
Leaves in panels	580
Flowers in panels	950 light
	3064 medium
	356 dark

KEY
☐ tone 1
▨ tone 2
▨ tone 3
▨ tone 4
▨ tone 5
■ tone 6

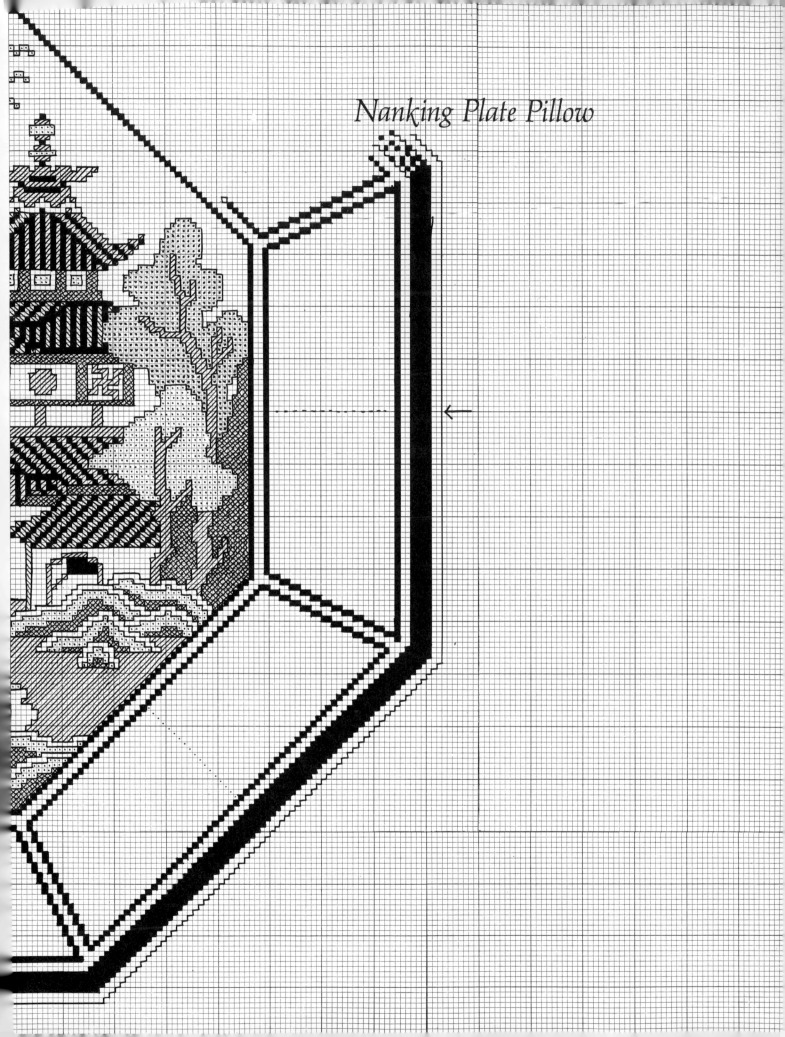

Nanking Plate Pillow

Nanking Plate Pillow

OCTAGON 17" in diameter

The square within which the octagon pillow fits measures 226 threads by 226 threads. Bind off a piece of #14 canvas measuring 21" by 21". Mark horizontal and vertical center lines. Outline square, then draw graph lines in work area.

Six tones are used in this design. They range from 1, light, to 6, dark.

The original pillow was made with D.M.C. cotton. The key to the colors used follows:

1. 3072 off-white
2. 809 light blue
3. 799 light medium blue
4. 798 medium blue
5. 797 dark medium blue
6. 820 dark blue

The graph has been drawn with tonal symbols in each square so no instructions are necessary for tonal placement *except:*
NOTE: Use #4 tone instead of #6 in the border around the eight border panels. Use #6, as shown, to outline border panels. (This note applies only to this design. The eight-panel frame for the Nanking Plate is also the frame for the following three pillows: the Dove, the Shrike, and the Magpie.)

The design was adapted from an antique Nanking saucer in my possession. (See photograph.) The designs in the border panels of the porcelain original were eliminated in favor of panels of decorative stitching. (I did, however, use the floral branch in the border panels for the Sung Dynasty Pair of Geese.)

In the original Nanking Plate pillow I also used decorative stitches throughout the face of the design. I used the Smyrna cross stitch for one tree, the star stitch for another, a square eyelet for

a third, and the upright cross stitch for a fourth. In the grass on the island to the right I used Hungarian ground, or Point d'Hongrie, and in the hill behind the trees on the right side I used the Florentine Mosaic stitch.

For the horizontal and vertical border panels I chose the leaf stitch, and the jacquard stitch for the diagonal panels. For symmetry's sake, I began the jacquard stitch in the center of each panel, and worked from there toward the ends of the panels. Thereafter I worked from one end of a panel to the other.

The pillow requires a 2″ fabric boxing. Match it to the #4 tone you have used in your pillow. Cut a strip 60″ in length and 3½″ in width. For complete instructions on applying boxing bands and backing, turn to p. 122.

Antique Nanking plate

Shrike Pillow

After a painting by Li An Chung, ca. 1110, Sung Dynasty. CHINESE NATIONAL PALACE MUSEUM. TAICHING, TAIWAN.

OCTAGON 17″ in diameter

THE square within which the octagon pillow fits measures 226 threads by 226 threads. Bind off a piece of #14 canvas measuring 21″ by 21″. Mark horizontal and vertical center lines. Outline square, then draw graph lines in work area. (Use Nanking Plate graph for outer frame.)

Twenty colors of D.M.C. cotton were used in the original pillow. The key to their numbers and their placement in the design follows:

645 dark taupe gray	Use for X'd shading on top of head, down back of neck, in upper wing; in circular area between upper back and upper breast; across lower back, i.e., at top of tail; and for lighter part of feet.
646 medium dark taupe gray	Use for slant-line shading on upper back; in circular area between upper back and upper breast; in upper wings; and across lower back, i.e., at top of tail.
647 medium taupe gray	Use for small x shading on head; back; upper wings and oval area under wing, i.e., on thigh.
648 light taupe gray	Use for dotted area at edge of puff on bird's back, dotted on graph.

3032 lightest gray	Use for dotted area at upper breast, under beak; for dotted oval area under wing, i.e., on thigh; and at upper end of under-tail.
782 burnt amber	Use for eyes and initials. (Use your own initials.)
Blanc neige, white	Use for all parts of the bird left white on graph.
420 tobacco	Use for beak.
3031 dark brown	Use for dark part of beak; for black areas in upper wings and between breast and shoulder puff; and for dark part of feet. Use 645 for lighter part of feet.
311 navy blue	Use for black area around eye; for black area on tail and lower wing; for outline of octagon; for outlines of eight panels and for shaded band next to pillow's edge.
312 medium dark blue 322 medium blue 334 medium light blue 3325 light blue	Use for shading lower wing up to thigh.
3011 olive brown	Use for two leafless branches, left white on graph.
649 lime green	Use for leaves with small x in shading.
937 medium sap green	Use for all leaves with diagonal shading.
934 dark green	Use for all leaves with large X shading.
613 chamois gold	Use for background.

Work the brick stitch within the inner octagon, i.e., around the bird. I use it turned over on its side. Work basket weave around and between eight panels, and for outer border. (Needless to say, use basket weave for bird, branches and leaves.)

For this pillow I used the double cross stitch in the horizontal and vertical panels, and the jacquard stitch in the diagonal panels. For symmetry's sake, begin the first row of the jacquard stitch at the center line on the diagonal panels. Work along the inner outline of the panel, from center to one end, then from center to the other end. Thereafter work from end to end.

The pillow requires a 2″ fabric boxing. Match it to 311 navy blue. Cut a strip 60″ in length and 3½″ in width. For complete instructions, turn to p. 122.

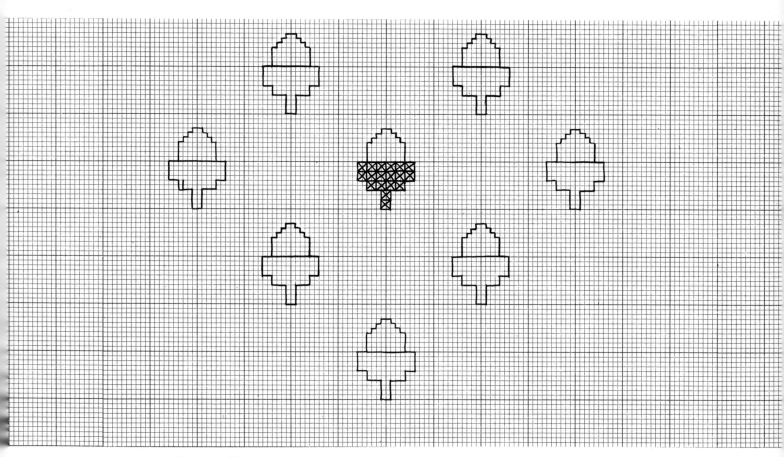

Acorn pattern designed by author for center part of oak leaf wreath on chair seats design for governor's mansion in Des Moines, Iowa.

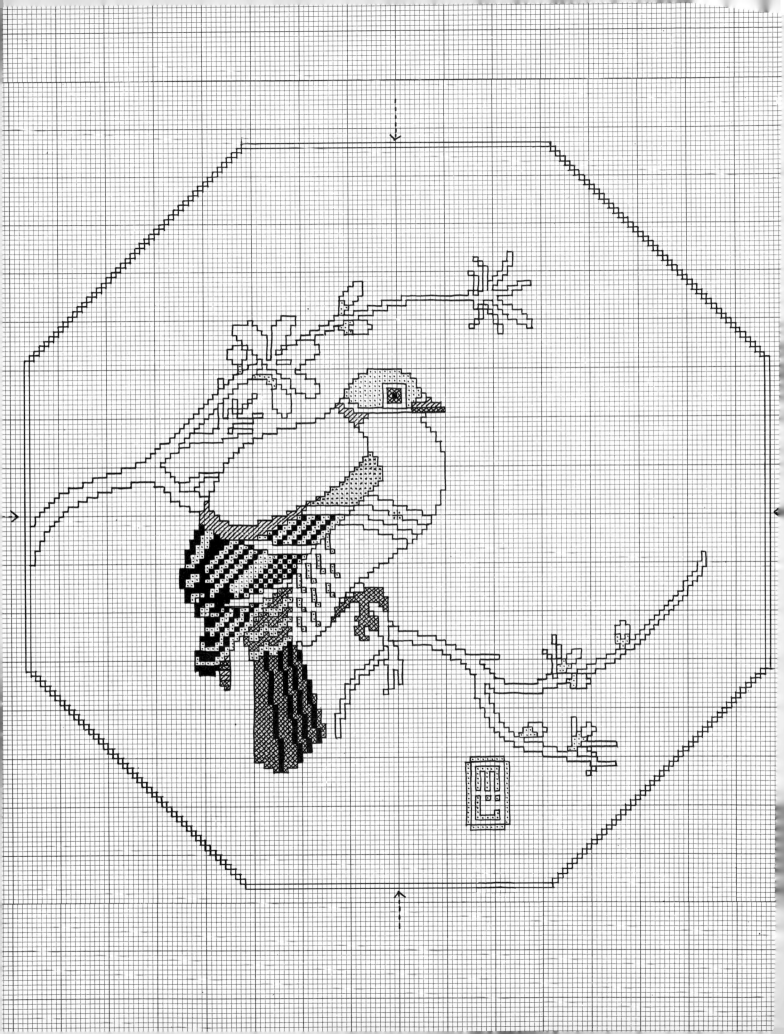

Dove at a Branch of Peach Blossoms

After a painting by Emperor Hui Tsung, Sung Dynasty.

OCTAGON 17″ in diameter

THE square within which the octagon pillow fits measures 226 threads by 226 threads. Bind off a piece of #14 canvas measuring 21″ by 21″. Mark horizontal and vertical center lines. Outline square, then draw graph lines in work area. (Use Nanking Plate graph for outer frame.)

Fourteen colors of D.M.C. cotton were used in the original pillow. The key to their numbers and their placement in the design follows:

926 medium teal blue	Use for top of head, dotted on graph; and upper part of beak, shaded on graph.
Blanc neige, white	Use for outline of eye; upper root of beak; buds and flowers; step 5 of breast, i.e., lower forward part of bird's body; and for two lower horizontal bands in wings.
645 dark gray	Use for dark line in beak; and for feet.
301 bitter-sweet	Use for shaded area in eye (iris is 3371 brown); and for initials. (Use your own.)
3052 gray-green	Use for 1st step of breast shading, i.e., large area under head; and for stems of flowers, dotted on graph.
3053 gray-green	Use for 2nd step of breast shading, i.e., top step of three shallow steps left white on graph; and for dotted lines in lower body.
3013 soft green-gold	Use for 3rd step of breast shading; and for BACKGROUND.

(133)

3072 pale gray-green	Use for 4th step of breast shading. (Fifth step under blanc neige.)
3011 olive	Use for shaded area at back of neck; and with 3021 brown for double cross stitch on bird's back, i.e., large unshaded areas. Outline first with brown, then work diagonal cross stitches in olive. Finally, fill in empty holes with upright cross stitches in brown. Use 3011 olive for shaded area between back and wing; for dotted areas in wings; and for three dotted bands in upper part of tail.
3021 brown	Use with 3011 olive in double cross stitch on back of bird; and for x'd areas in upper and lower tail.
3371 dark brown	Use for black areas in wing and tail; and for iris in eye.
640 fawn brown	Use for branches of trees.
3051 sage green	Use for outline of central octagon; outlines of eight border panels; and for shaded band in outer border, near edge of pillow.

Work the brick stitch within the inner octagon, i.e., around the bird and branches (all worked in basket weave). I use the brick stitch turned over on its side. Work the basket weave around and between panels, and for outer border.

For this pillow I used the same textured stitch for all eight octagon panels. My choice was the double straight cross stitch.

The pillow requires a 2" fabric boxing. Match it to 3051 sage green. Cut a strip 60" in length and 3½" in width. For complete instructions on applying boxing bands and backing, turn to p. 122.

Chinese Silkworm Moth Pillow

Nanking Plate Pillow

Sung Dynasty Geese

Foo Lion Pillow

Cloud Band Pillow

Anniversary Pillow

Adam and Eve

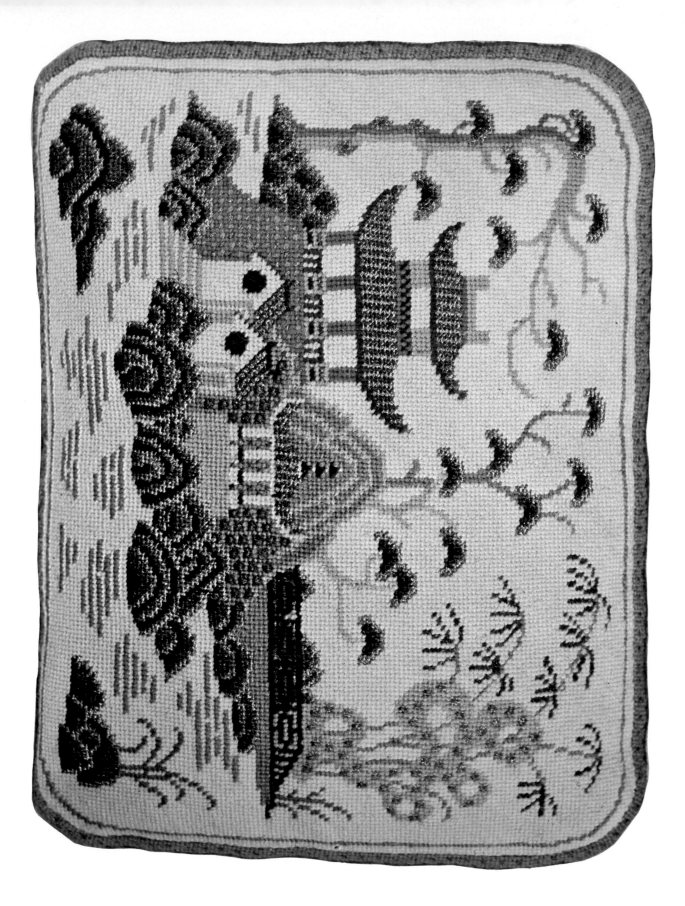

Scenic Pillow

Sternotomis Pulchra Beetle

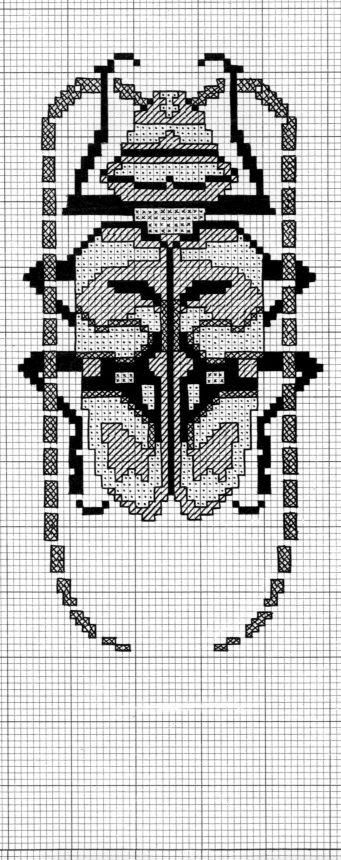

A Magpie on a Flowering Branch

Detail from a painting in the style of the Sung Dynasty. THE METROPOLITAN MUSEUM OF ART.

OCTAGON 17" in diameter

THE square within which the octagon pillow fits measures 226 threads by 226 threads. Bind off a piece of #14 canvas measuring 21" by 21". Mark horizontal and vertical center lines. Outline square, then draw graph lines in work area. (Use Nanking Plate graph for outer frame.)

Twenty tones and colors of French silk were used in the original pillow. The key to their numbers and their placement in the design follows:

2636 red for beak, claws and initials (Use your own initials.)
3414 medium gray in head and lower wings
3415 medium dark gray in head and lower wings
3416 dark gray in head and lower wings
2232 light gold for breast and tail
2234 medium gold for breast and tail
2235 dark gold for breast
3433 light mauve gray in upper wing
3434 medium mauve gray in upper wing
3435 dark mauve gray in upper wing
3845 dark gray spots in tail
3833 brown for branches
3834 darker brown for outlining branches
3723 light green for leaves
3724 medium green for leaves
3725 dark green for leaves
Blanc white for flowers in foreground. Work in double straight cross stitch.
3711 off-white in tail and white flowers in background. Work latter in double straight cross stitch.
3712 taupe background color
3713 darker taupe for outlining octagon panels and pillow

Petitpoint Envelope Handbag

Approximately 7″ by 10″ when closed

THE outer cover of the handbag measures 185 threads by 245 threads. Bind off a piece of #18 canvas measuring 14″ by 18″. Mark horizontal and vertical center threads. Outline work area, then draw graph lines within these outlines.

Six colors of Medici wool were used in the original bag. Their numbers follow:

> #1 tone blanc, white
> #2 tone 502 bis, beige
> #3 tone 204 bis, sky blue
> #4 tone 411 sage green
> #5 tone 403 dark green
> #6 tone 200 navy blue

The graph has been prepared with tonal symbols in each square so no instructions are necessary for tonal placement except that the field of the pillow is in navy, as is the background of the border band. Both were left white in the graph so you could read the graph lines.

The two side gussets, the inner panel and the bottom strip should be made in navy petitpoint. Outlines for the actual finished sizes of these pieces are given on pages 140 and 141 for you to trace and transfer to your canvas.

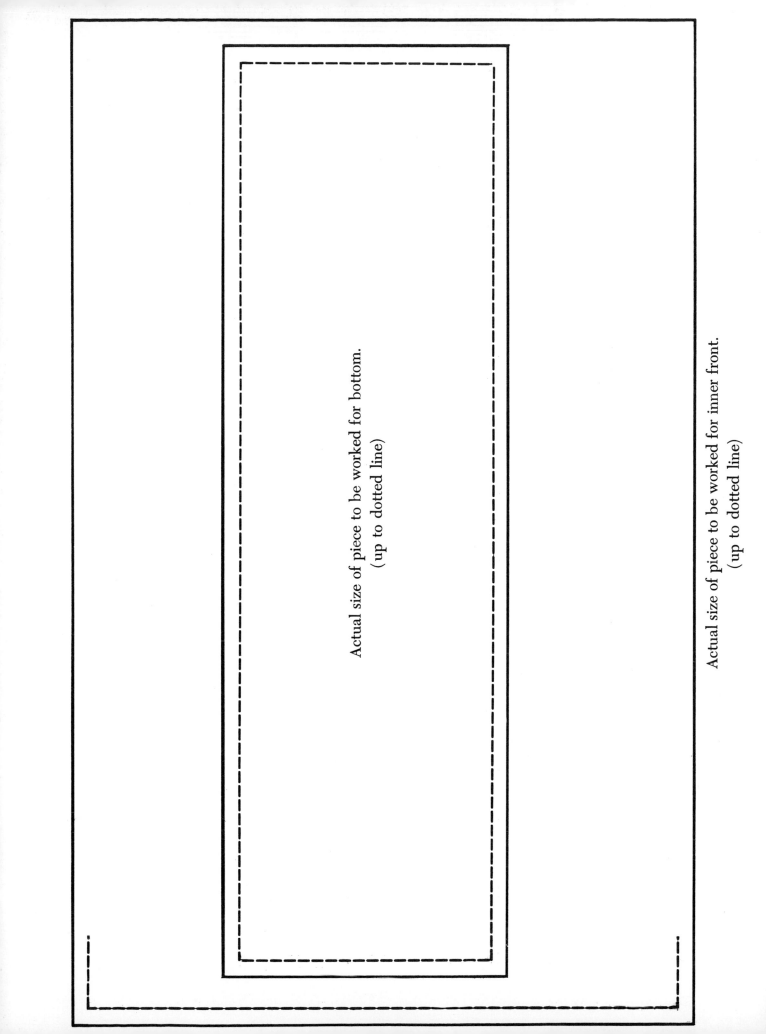

Actual size of piece to be worked for bottom.
(up to dotted line)

Actual size of piece to be worked for inner front.
(up to dotted line)

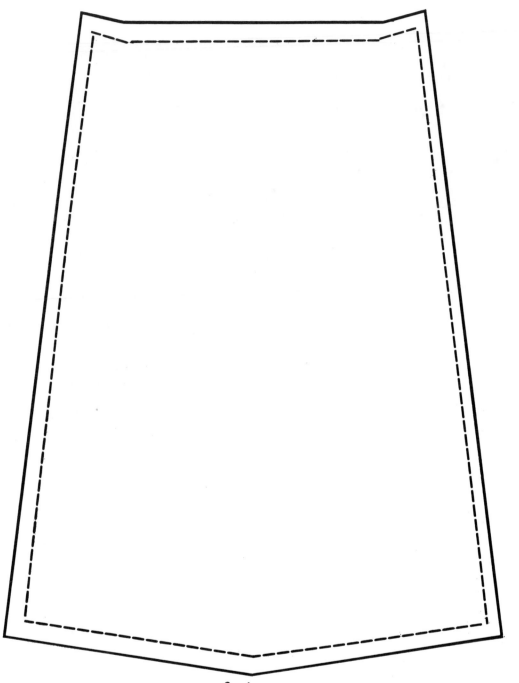

2 pieces

Actual size of 2 pieces to be worked for end gussets.
(up to dotted line)

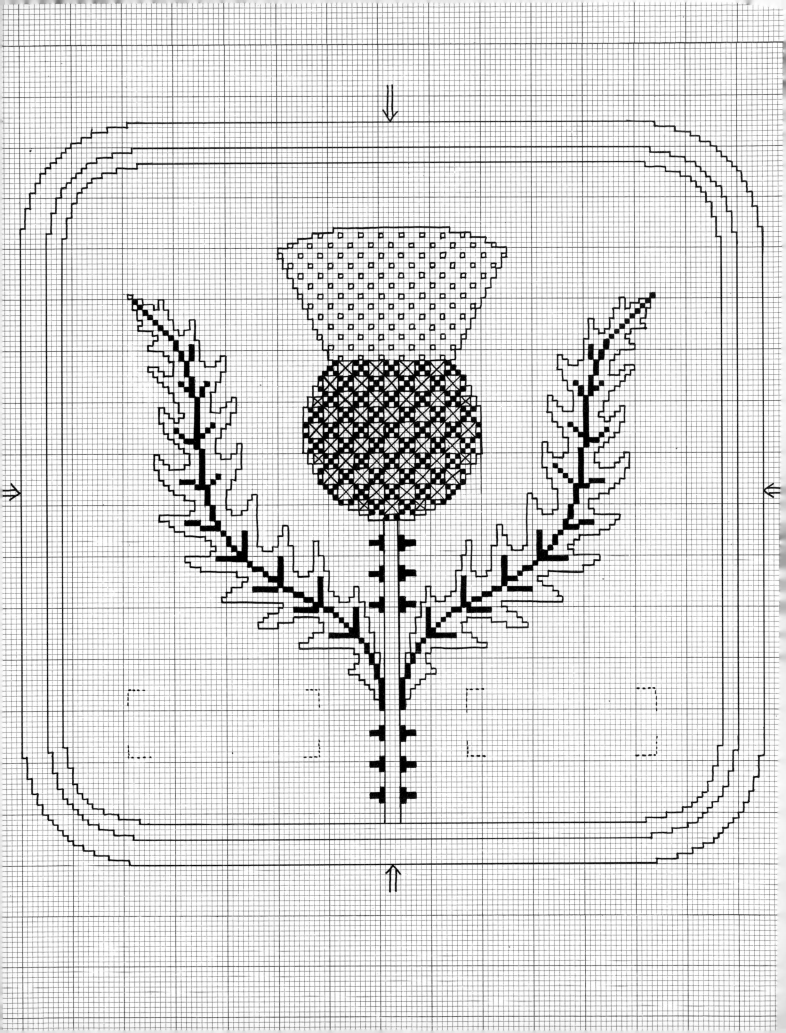

Thistle Pillow

12″ x 12″ x 1¾″

THE thistle pillow measures 145 threads by 145 threads. Bind off a piece of #12 canvas measuring 16″ by 16″. Outline work area, then draw graph lines within outline.

1) Using gold thread work the spines on the thistle stem, the veins of the leaves, and the diagonal lines in the bottom half of the flower, i.e., all black stitches on the graph.

2) Using white wool and a satin stitch, work the stem of the flower. Then outline the base of the thistle. Work triple cross stitches in base of flower, except the six Smyrna cross stitches where there is not room enough for the triple cross stitch. Using white wool, fill in flat stitches around the textured stitches.

3) Using white wool, outline upper part of thistle. Fill in with basket weave. Then, using three strands of white Persian wool, work over-stitches, following the pattern of small squares in the upper part of the flower.

4) Using white wool, outline and fill in leaves.

5) Using white wool work outline near pillow's edge.

6) Dates, in the two panels at either side of the stem, are optional. But if done should be in white wool.

7) Using a colored wool or silk, work brick stitch background.

8) Using the same colored wool or silk, work basketweave from white outline out to edge of pillow.

9) If you want to make a needlework boxing, bind off a piece of #12 canvas measuring 50″ by 6″. Count off 544 threads by 21 threads. Outline. Work your lettering out on graph paper. The letters should be 7 threads high and centered on the band, i.e., with 7 threads above and 7 below. Plan your lettering on the boxing so that the seam will be at bottom center.

Use your background color for the lettering. Use white for the background of the boxing band.

The letters on the last page of *Needlepoint by Design* are perfect for use here.

I made the pillow as a golden wedding gift for my parents. I used the thistle because my Father is Scottish. I worked it in white wool and gold thread. For the background, in honor of my parents' service as missionaries, I used silk of a color which the Chinese call "Sacrificial Red" (#636). On the banding the wording reads: "To Tirzah and Robert McCandliss on their Golden Anniversary, June 23rd." So you see you can put quite a legend on a boxing band.

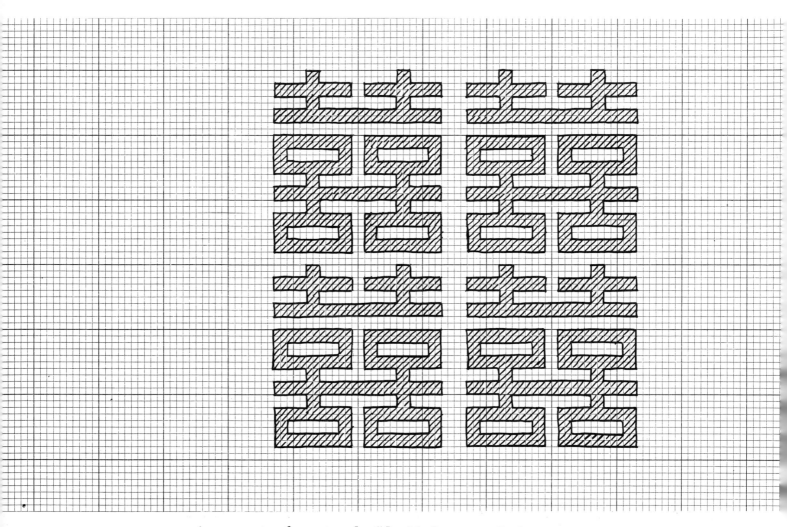

A suggestion for using the "double happiness" character as an all-over pattern.

Adam and Eve

OCTAGON 15½" in diameter

THE square within which the octagon pillow fits measures 208 threads by 208 threads. Bind off a piece of #14 canvas measuring 20" by 20". Mark horizontal and vertical center lines. Outline square, then draw graph lines in work area.

Three tones are used in the design:

1. Light
2. Medium
3. Dark

The original pillow was made with Medici wool. Key to colors used follows:

1. Blanc, white
2. 401 lime green
3. 200 navy blue

In D.M.C. cotton you might use:

1. Blanc neige, white
2. 581 lime green
3. 823 navy blue
   or
1. Blanc neige, white
2. 301 russet
3. 310 black

The graph has been prepared with tonal symbols in the design so no instructions are necessary for tonal placement.

The best way to work this design is to work first the #1 tone lines within the bodies and around each separate segment. Then fill in with #3 tone.

The eight panels in the border should be filled in with decorative stitches. I used the leaf stitch in the horizontal and

This graph has been cut down the center axis.

vertical panels, and the jacquard stitch in the diagonal panels. If you use the jacquard stitch, for symmetry's sake, BEGIN THE FIRST ROW IN THE CENTER OF THE PANEL AND WORK OUT TOWARD EACH END OF THE PANEL. I have made a dotted line in the graph to mark the center of the panels. After you have worked your first row in this way you will find it easy to begin each succeeding row at the end.

This pillow design was adapted from an Egyptian fourth century design from the E. Kofler-Truniger collection in Lucerne. Originally Venus and Adonis, the two figures became Adam and Eve when I put a serpent in her hands and an apple in one of his.

While sitting in my dentist's chair one day, I could only listen while the doctor talked about needlepoint. The subject of my first book came up, and then he said: "I know one sure fact, and it's sad: Hollywood will NEVER buy your book in order to make a movie of it. There's no sex in it!"

I signaled to him that I had something to say. He took his hands out of my mouth so I could speak.

"Ah, but you should see the pillow I'm working on now!" I said. "It's a design of two almost naked people. Don't you think I might conceivably arouse Hollywood's interest if I put a picture of this latest pillow on the cover of my second book and called it *Pornopoint?*"

The pillow requires a 2″ fabric boxing. Match it to the #2 tone. Cut a strip 52″ in length and 3½″ in width. For complete instructions on applying boxing bands and backing, turn to p. 122.

Bibliography

HANLEY, HOPE *Needlepoint,* New York, Charles Scribner's Sons, 1964.

DE DILLMONT, THERESE *Encyclopedia of Needlework,* France, D.M.C. Library.

SNOOK, BARBARA *Needlework Stitches,* New York, Crown, 1963.

LANE, MAGGIE *Needlepoint by Design,* New York, Charles Scribner's Sons, 1970.

SNOOK, BARBARA *Florentine Embroidery,* New York, Charles Scribner's Sons, 1967.

Index of Stitches